CU00842062

Someone You Love is Gay

How to Reconcile Your Faith with Homosexuality

Dr. Brandon Park

Copyright © 2022 Dr. Brandon Park & Park Enterprises, LLC
All rights reserved.

ACKNOWLEDGEMENTS

Special thanks to Paul Hart for designing the cover for this book.

Paul specializes in all types of graphic design, photography, and content development.

To hire Paul Hart for one of your media projects, visit his website:

www.PaulHart.io

CONTENTS

PROLOGUE

"To be loved but not known is comforting but superficial. To be known and not loved is our greatest fear. But to be fully known and truly loved is, well, a lot like being loved by God. It is what we need more than anything. It liberates us from pretense, humbles us out of our self-righteousness, and fortifies us for any difficulty life can throw at us."
— Tim Keller

Someone you love is gay. It's an emphatic statement because it's true. Those identifying as LGBTQ now comprise 5.6% of the U.S. population of adults. That means one out of every twenty people you come across is gay. Many are open about it; many are still hiding in the closet out of fear of what their loved ones would think.

This book was given to you because your gay loved one wants to be accepted and understood by you. I've had several friends tell me that this content encapsulates everything they've ever wanted to say to their family. It's what they've desired their loved ones to know about their sexuality from their point of view and how they have come to terms with it. So perhaps your gay loved one has given you this book. They've likely done so because they want you to enter their reality and experience the world through their eyes. The true essence of love is the recognition of yourself in another person. It's been eloquently said, "Love is the discovery of ourselves in others, and the delight in that recognition." It is seeing what they see and feeling as they feel.

Which is essentially what God did for us. Through Jesus, God stepped out of the realms of Heaven and into human form. He experienced life as we understand it. So my thoughtful challenge to you today is to do just the same. Be like Jesus and enter into the perspective of your loved one... who just so happens to be gay.

> The highest form of intelligence is the ability to observe without evaluating.

An ancient philosopher once said that the highest form of intelligence is the ability to observe without evaluating. So I'd encourage you to read this book as if you were watching and analyzing a new perspective — and wait until you get to the last chapter before making any judgment. What would it look like to drop all of your preconceived and fixed ideas about what you've thought about homosexuality and be neutral just for a moment?

One of the prayers that I pray every day when I first wake up is simply this: "God, lead me to discover Truth and help me to discern error." Personally, I believe that God continues to answer that prayer for me. As a result, I find more peace and joy in my life as my experience becomes congruent with my understanding of Scripture. I would encourage you to pray that same prayer and ask God to lead you to truth. For too long, Christians have only parroted the same-old traditional talking points on this issue without giving any other interpretation a fair hearing.

So I encourage you to read with an open mind. Consider the possibility that there could be another way of looking at this issue. Even if you don't theologically agree in the end, you'll still gain exceptional clarity regarding your gay loved one's life experience. A mark of an open mind is being more committed to your curiosity than to your convictions. The goal of learning is not to shield old views against new facts. It's to revise old views to incorporate new facts. Ideas are possibilities to explore, not certainties to defend.

The hallmark of an open mind is not letting your ideas become your identity. For things to reveal themselves to us as they really are, we need to be ready to abandon our preconceived notions about them. If you define yourself by your opinions, questioning them is a threat to your integrity. But if you see yourself as a curious person or a lifelong learner, changing your mind is an opportunity for growth.

If the church's teachings result in families being split apart and gay Christian teens committing suicide -- maybe it's time we reevaluate those teachings and ask if maybe there's something we might be missing?

One recent conversation I had became the catalyst for writing this book. I was meeting with a friend for dinner one night at Texas Roadhouse. We'll call him John (although that's not his real name). I was curious to hear John's story of how he came out and reconciled his strong faith in God with his sexual orientation. John had a similar background as I did. Growing up in the Baptist church, he became deeply devoted to God. Eventually, John served as a full-time missionary for a brief season overseas. However, soon after returning home from the mission field in his mid-20's, he informed his parents of something he couldn't hide any longer. He came out to his parents and told them he was gay. Like many Christian parents hearing this news, their reaction was not favorable or supportive in any way. John was immediately kicked out of his family home, and he went to spend the night at a friend's house. The next day his parents contacted him and said that he needed to pick up his belongings. What devastated my heart was hearing what happened next. His Mom and Dad had taken everything that belonged to him: clothes, shoes, personal belongings, pictures… even his baby blanket and baby shoes, and laid everything out in the driveway and along the sidewalk in front of their home for him to pick up. They didn't even want him back inside the house. He said what broke his heart the most was that his parents were disposing of all of the keepsakes they had when he was a baby. He felt like his sexual orientation was such a disgrace to his parents that they apparently felt the need to remove any evidence that he was ever their son.

> Having a gay child doesn't mean you failed as a parent. Disowning your gay child does mean you failed as a parent.

Hearing John's story as we sat across that table stirred something within me. Even though he and his parents had since reconciled, I could still sense the deep wound this had caused. Unfortunately, his story is not an isolated one. I've heard the same narrative repeated countless times. Gay Christian young people are being kicked out of their homes, with many never speaking to their families again. Having a gay child doesn't mean you failed as a parent; disowning your gay child does mean you failed as a parent. Although I didn't know his parents, I knew the church very well. Their education on this issue was identical to the same teaching that I also helped propagate as a pastor: homosexuality was a sin and an abomination against God. I felt a wave of remorse as I was reminded of how I had used my limited interpretation of Scripture to bring undue judgment against the LGBTQ community. I felt that anyone who believed differently from my traditional interpretation were just people looking for loopholes rather than just accepting the plain sense of Scripture. I had preached sermons against homosexuality. I had held press conferences, written articles for the newspaper, done countless TV news interviews speaking out against gay marriage, and even once appeared on a talk show -- all while secretly dealing with my own suppressed same-sex attraction to men.

I now felt a sense of responsibility to undo some of the damage I had done. What better person to advocate for this issue than someone who used to be such an outspoken proponent for the other side. I knew I needed to write and explain another valid interpretation of these Scriptures that doesn't twist the Bible into making it say what we want it to say. If more Christians knew the truth, we would stop weaponizing the Bible against the LGBTQ community.

I can now say that I have been on both polar opposite sides of this issue. I'm pretty confident I could outperform my opposition on their own talking points about this issue in a debate setting. As a pastor, I judged homosexuality so firmly and harshly because I was also judging myself. I subconsciously believed that doing so would keep me in check and that I would prove to God by my adamant devotion that this "sin" wasn't a part of me.

I'm writing this book for three reasons:

First, I'm writing to parents, siblings, grandparents, aunts, and uncles who have a loved one who is gay. Maybe you recently found out, or perhaps you've suspected it their whole life. You may be afraid for your gay loved one's soul and their eternal future. I validate your concern. I have a lot of compassion for parents who have pastors who were once like me. They are hearing from the pulpits that their gay child is an abomination in the eyes of God and

> Most Christians aren't trying to be homophobic. They're just trying to be faithful to their understanding of Scripture.

that they are living in a lifestyle of sin. Most pastors I know are sincere and lovable people who have the purest of intentions. Their convictions are Bible-based, and they want to protect the souls of those within their influence. So, of course, this must be the only correct and clear teaching from the Word of God. The reality is, most Christians aren't trying to be homophobic. They're just trying to be faithful to their understanding of Scripture. Parents are going to be fearful for the spiritual well-being of their gay kids. Their fear of your rejection combined with fear of being abandoned by God is an unholy cocktail that results in immense mental, emotional and spiritual damage. If there's another way of looking at this issue Scripturally, shouldn't we give that interpretation a fair hearing? Should we be more loyal to our preconceived ideas than we are to the people we love? This book is for anyone who wonders, even subconsciously: *Has the church obsessed over this too much? Do we really think we've gotten it right?* Perhaps there's no greater gift you can give to your loved one than the gift of finally being understood. People don't need another human being to make their life complete, but let's be honest. Having your wounds embraced by someone who doesn't see them as disasters in your soul but rather as cracks to put their love into is the most calming thing in the world. That's what your loved one needs from you in this moment.

Secondly, I'm writing this book for those who are part of the LGBTQ community but have felt like you've had no other choice but to walk away from faith entirely — believing that God has no place at the table for you. The Christian who struggles with homosexuality faces a perilous dilemma: Do I give up being Christian because I am gay? So many gay people have abandoned their Christian beliefs because they cannot reconcile the unchangeable reality of who they are with what they were brought up to believe. Many falsely believe that accepting that you are gay severs any connection with the divine. As a result, you and God aren't exactly on speaking terms anymore. Many of you are angry with God because He didn't answer your prayers to make you straight, and you blame Him for causing your life to be in continual conflict. One friend once confessed to me, "Why should I communicate with a God who'd ignored my cries for help and let me down." This book is for those of you who have walked away from the Church, yet you're still secretly into Jesus and always will be. My prayer is that God will guide you into

> Many of you are angry with God because He didn't answer your prayers to make you straight.

integrating all parts of yourself — mental, spiritual, sexual, physical — so that you will finally feel whole. After all, the Greek word for salvation is *sozo*, which means "to heal, bring wholeness, to preserve." This is what God wants to do in your life. To heal the fractured parts of yourself back together into integrated wholeness.

The third reason I'm writing this book is for myself. It's cathartic and healing for me to share my story with others. This is my attempt to make peace with my past and journal my journey. Even as I've written, there have been so many moments where I've had to stop to grab a tissue and wipe the tears from my eyes. This book has resurfaced my deepest wounds and my most painful emotions. For years, I'd purposely left many of these memories behind but now was being forced to face them again with every agonizing and heart-wrenching detail. Sometimes giving words to those painful experiences allows you to finally grieve and release them. Ironically, in one regard, this has been the easiest book I've ever chosen to write. From start to finish, I wrote this entirety in just a few weeks. I think it's because I've thought about this issue and wrestled with this topic nearly every day for the last 40 years. I have a lot of insight to give to this topic.

I don't know about you, but I get clarity through writing. Dawson Trotman used to say, "Thoughts disentangle themselves through the lips and through the fingertips." When we're not speaking it, we're storing it…and that stuff gets real heavy real quick. But we gain clarity and understanding about ourselves, make sense of our past, and gain wisdom for the future when we talk it out and write it out.

> Those parts of you that you are most fearful of disclosing are the very parts that will be most helpful to others if you are willing to admit them.

My life experience has taught me that those parts of you that you are most fearful of disclosing are the very parts that will be the most helpful to others if you are willing to admit them. Opening up about your struggles helps people so much more than talking about your strengths. People may be somewhat inspired when you share your successes with them, but they connect with you (and feel less alone) when you share your failures with them.

This book is perhaps my first opportunity to be publicly honest with who I am. So writing this is admittedly therapeutic for someone who has lived his whole life obsessed with personal image and what people think about me.

I honestly didn't want to write this book, and I struggled reluctantly about sharing these thoughts for almost three years. I'm a very private person, and for me, there's nothing that should be more private than your sexuality. I also don't want my life to be known and labeled for my sexual orientation. Talking about sexual orientation issues is *not* my calling or purpose in life. Unfortunately, it seems as if when people find out about someone being gay, they don't think of them or treat them the same way ever again. The stigma of being perceived by others as gay is a perception that follows you for the rest of your life. You can't come back from that.

I write this at the risk of now carrying that stigma. Facing my truth and owning my story meant that I might hurt my family and those I love the most by becoming an object of embarrassment, ridicule, and shame. I risk being misunderstood by others. Many will make judgments and assumptions about me based on their own preconceived ideas and prejudices.

Yet I'm reminded of a statement made years ago. In 1978, Harvey Milk of San Francisco was the first openly gay elected official in the United States. Harvey repeatedly said to the gay community: "Come out, and when you do, you will feel so much better." Before he was assassinated in 1979, Harvey predicted that he would be murdered, but he said that he would gladly take a bullet if it would blast open all of the closet doors that trap and imprison people. I believe that receiving the bullet of backlash and personal criticism is a very small price for me to pay if it saves families from being torn apart and brings the gay community to a personal knowledge of God.

Most of my life was spent pleasing others by saying and doing the things they wanted, but deep down, I knew I wasn't living true to myself. I'm now no longer denying the reality of my inner-being. I accept who I am, and I refuse to receive any attempts to make me feel ashamed of myself. Those days of living in shame are over.

If there's anything I've learned in recent years, it's simply this: the best weight you'll ever lose is the weight of other people's opinion of you. Dr. Seuss said it best: "Be who you are and say what you feel because those who mind don't matter and those

> The best weight you'll ever lose is the weight of other people's opinion of you.

who matter don't mind." Your life isn't yours if you always care about what others think. As one comedian put it, "I used to care what people thought about me until one day I tried to pay my bills with their opinions."

I find the words of Audrey Kitching reassuring:

> I think something people need to understand is that others disliking you is not a bad thing. When you are embodying your true authentic self, it creates fear in people who still operate from the ego. If you want to grow, heal, and evolve, you have to let go of wanting to be liked.

I know that my story could be the key that unlocks someone else's prison. My painful experiences aren't wasted if someone can learn and benefit from them. Therefore I have an obligation to share it. As Brene Brown said, "One day, you will tell your story of how you overcame what you went through and it will be someone else's survival guide."

This is my story…

THE RISE AND FALL OF A MEGACHURCH PASTOR

"You're allowed to be disappointed. You're allowed to be angry. You're allowed to be scared. You're allowed to cry. But... you are not allowed to give up."
— Anonymous

"How do I painlessly end my life?" Those were the words I typed into my Google search browser through eyes that could barely see through the tears. The agony I felt made it difficult to even breathe. The pain and grief I was experiencing felt so crippling that I was confident I couldn't bear to live with it any longer. The decision had been made that I needed to begin putting my affairs in order and implement what would be the exit plan of my life. I had made a list of what needed to be done. Establishing a trust for my children; writing letters to each of the kids to be opened on special days; getting rid of unused items so my family wouldn't have as much to sort through after I was gone. And I had now done enough research to know exactly how many pills I would need to swallow of a specific medication in order to fall asleep and never wake up again.

Often I would look back and wonder about the series of events that had led to this breaking point. I have always felt different from other boys from as early as I can remember. From lunch tables to locker rooms, I had long thought that I marched to the beat of a different masculine drum. Then, as puberty hit full bloom, my pull towards guys frighteningly turned into genuine sexual attraction — although, at the time, my sheltered mind had no idea what a gay person was or that they even existed. All I knew was that I was different. I feared that there was something wrong with me. I'll never forget the day in middle school when I connected who I was with what homosexuality is. A sheer wave of absolute panic swept over me. That thought-turned-feeling reverberated throughout my entire body. "*What if I really am a faggot?*" I thought to myself. "*And what if this never goes away?*" Shame, embarrassment, anger, rage, and sadness enveloped my whole being. No one would ever choose to be queer; it was a sinister act of nature to me. My worst fear became my most suppressed reality. Homosexuals were destined to a life of rejection, and if by some wicked twist of fate a person was one, they must do everything possible to conceal it from everyone else. This early need for secrecy becomes the subconscious motivator in nearly every gay man's life.

Puberty is hard enough on anyone, but throw in same-sex attraction on an insecure, scrawny kid with cystic acne and major anxiety issues, and it was practically unbearable. I made the decision that I would not be gay and that, with God's help, I would do everything within my power to overcome this. I would "pray the gay away" -- and I knew that God would answer any prayer that was prayed in accordance to His will! I sincerely believed that if I prayed hard enough and showed God my devotion to change, He would deliver me from these "evil" desires and replace them with a pure and holy heterosexual orientation.

From as early as I could remember, I was romantically and emotionally attracted to women while sexually attracted to men. I always dreamed of getting married and having a wife and at least three kids one day. In my mind, I wasn't going to allow Satan to use this to take me away from that dream and what I felt was God's purpose for my life.

My family and I went to church every Sunday. We were a picturesque Southern Baptist family of four. The Parks were in church every time the doors were open…and I mean that literally. When our church in Stuart, Florida, began to grow, our pastor decided to have two identical Sunday morning worship services. I remember being in the car when my sister and I asked Dad which service we would be going to. His answer: "Both of them!" I chuckle looking back on that memory. We were devoted to our church and our God. Our faith was the epicenter of our home, and even though I didn't care for church much as a kid, I grew to love it in my teenage years.

I feel so blessed to have had been raised by people like my Mom and Dad. They truly are amazing parents and I love them with all my heart. They've only wanted what was best for my sister and I and they truly did everything they could to "raise us right." Dad worked hard as a lineman for the local power company and mom worked as a property appraiser for the local government. We were a typical, middle-class family who loved God and others to the best of our ability.

My adolescence was so immersed in my Christian subculture of the 1990's complete with Jesus fish charms, WWJD bracelets, T-shirts with catchy (and sometimes cheesy) Christian slogans, and the complete set of every Amy Grant, dc Talk, and Newsboys album.

The 1990s were also known (at least in the evangelical Christian world) for the rise of the Purity Movement. *I Kissed Dating Goodbye* by Joshua Harris was the book that literally every teen in my youth group was reading. Dating was considered too risky for those who were truly devoted to God. We were told to never put any relationship ahead of Him, which honestly fostered a fear of intimacy right away. The purity movement was bolstered with purity rings, a True Love Waits pledge card, any book by Dr. James Dobson, and multiple repetitions of dc Talk's song, "I Don't Want It" on youth group road trips. I was scared to even talk to girls, let alone try to have a girlfriend because an inappropriate relationship could "lead me to sin" and cause me to miss God's plan for my life.

As a response to the purity culture of my teenage years, I had made the decision that not only would I remain a virgin until I got married but that I would also not even kiss a girl until the day I asked her to marry me. This was very convenient for me as I didn't have to deal with my lack of sexual response to females. And the thought of someday having a girlfriend by my side would demonstrate to me that God had really healed me of my same-sex attraction.

Having grown up in a Southern Baptist church, I was overly familiar with our interpretation of what the Bible said about homosexuality. My understanding had always been that anyone who was thought to be "that way" was an abomination before God. For evangelical Christians, "gay" wasn't a word we could ever use to describe ourselves. That was something that only lost people are saved from. It was still a foreign concept for me because it was a label with which we could never identify. As a Christian, I believed I could *not* be gay. There had to be some other reason why I had these feelings. How could I reconcile that I was born-again and made a new creation in Christ, yet this issue seemed to be at the core of who I was, and it wasn't going anywhere?

I knew I was different from as early as I could remember, but I couldn't quite put the finger on it as to why. I was also very homophobic growing up… and even in my early adult years as a pastor. I did everything I could to hide and suppress this part of myself, and I tried my hardest to come across as masculine as possible.

> Those who are the most homophobic are likely repressing their own same-sex desires.

I've since learned that those who are the most homophobic in this world are actually individuals who themselves are repressing their own same-sex desires. Research shows that people who internalize or deny their homosexuality often vent anger and disgust on other gay people. They manifest and project their own internalized homophobia by treating gay people as the object or target of their own shame. What's not a part of us doesn't bother us. The hatred and disgust we project onto others is really just a mirror of the hatred and disgust we feel within ourselves. Homophobia is nothing more than the outward manifestation of repressed homosexuality. I know it because that's what I used to do. Have you ever noticed how we, as Christians, are so often a bunch of pots and kettles pointing out the flaws in others that we are just as guilty of ourselves? The flip side of that equation is also true. Everything that irritates us about others can lead to a deeper understanding of ourselves.

Growing up with these desires made me think and feel two ways about God simultaneously. I believed (on the surface anyway) that God loved me unconditionally and that He had a plan and purpose for my life. Yet equally, I felt judged and condemned for having these desires and feeling trapped by the sin that enveloped me.

If the topic of homosexuals ever came up in church, they were always lumped into the same category as thieves, murderers, adulterers, and pedophiles. Whether or not homosexuality was a sin was never up for debate. It was a non-starter. As a result, I never bothered to investigate any other interpretations of these Scriptures different than the one rehashed within our own evangelical echo chamber. The Bible was clear, I thought. And anyone who tried to teach or believe otherwise was doing "exegetical gymnastics" around the Scriptures.

> Other people had sin struggles... but mine was abhorrent to God.

I began to fear that if these desires never went away, then it must mean that I wasn't genuinely saved. In the church that I grew up in, it was very common for everyone to question their salvation. It seemed like every member of our church got baptized more than once. "If you are 99% certain of your salvation, then you are 100% lost" was one of the talking points that led people to keep coming forward to the altar to be re-saved and re-baptized. There was no room for doubt or questioning your salvation when your eternity in heaven or hell was at stake. I had "prayed the sinner's prayer" more times than I can remember, and I was baptized twice. But my struggle never went away, and soon after, the doubts about where I stood in relation to God would come like a flood. It felt as though there was something very wrong with me. Maybe I wasn't trying hard enough, praying hard enough, or surrendering enough. My "sin issue" was perceived differently in my mind than everyone else's sin in the church. Other people had sin struggles... but mine was abhorrent to God. He despised it, and if I didn't get it dealt with, then God would inevitably despise me. Deep down, I just never felt that God could love someone who was as screwed up as I thought I was as a child. I felt I was unlovable and unworthy of God's love.

These factors contributed to the intense anxiety and worry that would become the running theme of my teenage years. My health took a hit as a teenager. I was painfully thin and had a hard time eating much of the time. My anxious mind caused me to not have much of an appetite, and I struggled to keep weight on.

After I made the decision to follow Jesus and be baptized (for the last time), I knew that I loved Jesus with my whole heart. I spent my free time as a 13-year-old learning about Jesus and how he taught me to live. I even asked Mom to buy me a book on theology because I wanted to know God better. Everything about me seemed to have changed — except for this one particular issue. I often thought that if only I could rid myself of same-sex attraction, then I'd literally be able to live a sin-free life. Of course, I knew that wasn't true, and I knew I had many other issues to work on as I grew in my discipleship process. But this solitary issue seemed to be so large and immutable that any other vice I may have had paled in comparison.

As a teenager, I became the poster child for ministry. When I was 14 years old, two other friends and I started an on-campus Bible study called OFC (On Fire for Christ). I began organizing prayer groups, teaching Bible Studies, and helping put on evangelistic events to save all my friends. I preached my first sermon in "big church" when I was 14 years old — a sermon on "How to Overcome Worry" from Matthew 6. It was a relevant topic for me because I struggled daily with anxiety. I literally worried about everything, and many times, my anxious thoughts even prevented me from eating, studying, and functioning normally. Looking back, I probably should have been medicated, but that was unheard of for kids in the 1990s.

When I made that decision at the age of 14 to "surrender to the call of ministry" and become a pastor, I truly wanted to make a difference in other people's lives and help them become all that God meant for them to be. Yet deep down, there was a secondary and shadowy motivation for wanting to go into ministry. I thought that if I could do something big enough for God, then He would accept me despite this "problem" that I had. I could prove that I was worthy enough of His love, and what better way to do that than to be a pastor. He would then love the unlovable me. That if I could be good enough, live perfect enough, preach well enough, and make a difference significant enough — that I would finally be deserving of His love and acceptance.

All throughout my teenage years, it was more of the same. I taught Sunday School every week throughout my high school years, worked at a Christian Bookstore every day after school, and volunteered at my church to do "soul-winning" visitation. Then, at the age of 18, I was ordained and began preaching in small churches. During that year, I also started a radio ministry called *The Divine Connection* that aired on a local FM station and preached on TBN — Trinity Broadcast Network television.

At the age of 19, I pastored my first church. And I continued pastoring for the next 19 years serving churches in rural Virginia, South Florida, and Missouri. I had earned two master's degrees and a doctorate in seminary. In 2007, we moved to Miami, Florida, where I pastored for the next 5 years and saw that church double in size as it grew from 400 to 800 in attendance each Sunday. I later pastored a megachurch in the suburbs of Kansas City. Those were exciting years as we were featured in *Outreach Magazine's* list of the "Top 100 Fastest-Growing Churches in America" and eventually added new services, new staff, new ministries, and a second campus in a neighboring city.

Every week, I received encouraging letters and emails from people who had been positively impacted by my ministry. I had no explanation for why God anointed my ministry or why my talent continued to grow, or why people's lives continued to be changed because of my teaching. It didn't make any sense to me at all. Everything about me felt different except for the part of me that brought the biggest shame. That never changed and never went away. In spite of it, I just surrendered to being used by God to the best of my ability. I just assumed that God had entrusted me with this "thorn in the flesh" for a reason because maybe He knew I could handle it. I wasn't going to let him down, my family down, or my church down. I had learned to compartmentalize my secret life from my public life. There was a split between what I was showing to the world and who I really was. I had grown so accustomed to having this lack of congruency or life integration that it seemed like a way of life for me.

I went to a Christian college that Dr. Jerry Falwell had founded in Lynchburg, Virginia — Liberty University. It was there that I met the remarkable woman who would later become my wife. She was a beautiful, attractive girl with a fun-loving personality who actually had an interest in me. I had always thought that if I had just met the right woman, it would "change" me. And if I could marry such a woman, then I'd always be a straight man and never have to deal with this issue again. Getting married would be the solution that would forever fix me.

> I had always thought that if I had just met the right woman, it would "change" me.

I can totally resonate with something said by Colton Underwood, the NFL and star of The Bachelor reality tv series, who recently came out as gay. In his Netflix series *Coming Out Colton*, he remarked that "The night that Cassie was leaving me on The Bachelor, there was a big part of me that was thinking, 'If I can't get there with you then I definitely can't with any other woman.'" That's how I felt about meeting and marrying my wife as well.

I had always thought that if I could just find the right woman to marry, then that would certainly be the "missing piece to take away the gay." After all, that's how it was supposed to work. If you "saved yourself for marriage," one was guaranteed to have an amazing and rewarding sex life replete with God's blessing on your relationship. I loved my wife dearly. Even to this day, I have nothing but admiration and respect for her. She's truly a loving and authentic person and an unbelievably good mother to our kids. Yet something was always missing in our marriage. There wasn't as much of a "spark" or chemistry in our relationship. My own shame and deep core hatred for myself would ensure that we would never deeply connect. Sure, there were moments when we did have that spark, even strongly at times — but they were few and far between. It was more like we were best friends raising our three beautiful kids together. It wasn't what I had hoped marriage would be, but I was content to settle for that. I always thought, "It's more important that we love each other. That's all that matters."

When we first got married, we went to a conference for pastors and their wives hosted by my mentor in the ministry — Dr. Adrian Rogers. Adrian and his wife Joyce had shared how one of the things they would do with each other was to exchange this little stuffed animal back and forth between the two of them. The couples at this conference were each given a small teddy bear holding a heart that said, "I love you." It was something that Carrie and I had given to each other countless times. If I were going on a trip, she would pack it in my suitcase. I would often hide it under her pillowcase. We'd sometimes get pretty creative in leaving it in surprising locations where the other would find it. That little stuffed bear grew to have a lot of sentimental value in our home.

I enjoyed being married to her and raising our precious little children together. Deep down, I had just assumed that my secret struggle was just something I would need to take with me to my grave. I knew full well how she felt about the "gay issue." It was no different than how I felt about it. I knew that if she knew me as I knew myself, she would undoubtedly divorce me. This wasn't something she had signed up for. For me to fully expose my deepest secret meant that I would lose my marriage, my kids, my home, and I'd lose my job as well (because a career in ministry is predicated on having a good marriage). Not only that, but I had also learned how to compartmentalize my sexuality and repress it with great skill. I lived most of my life in a state of denial about it myself. I was as honest with her as I could be with myself.

When my wife and I found out that we were pregnant with our firstborn, a boy, I began staying up late at night reading and researching if there was anything I could do as a father to ensure that my son would not turn out like his Dad and deal with the same struggle. I was falsely taught that homosexuality was a preventable disorder. Now I know that there is no scientific evidence to back that claim up. It's not a disorder any more than heterosexuality is a disorder.

One of my biggest fears as a parent was that one of my own children would be gay. Of course, in our circles, that was every parent's nightmare. I certainly didn't want to become that source of embarrassment or shame to my parents if they found this out about me.

I started reading books and studying reparative therapy. I even secretly started seeing a Christian therapist who I thought would help me finally rid myself of this unwanted same-sex attraction. I was told that if I could just get enough good male friends, my emotional needs would be met, and the gay would go away. After spending hundreds of dollars for each session, it all left me in a worse place financially and emotionally. Nothing was working. Nothing was changing. And when I shared with him these frustrations, his response was that I simply wasn't trying hard enough. I left feeling more despair than I did when I went in. After a half dozen sessions or so, I stopped going.

It took me about 35 years before I could share my deepest secret with another human being who wasn't a counselor — a guy who was the closest friend I've ever had. He was the one I felt like I could trust with my life. I remember feeling so scared being that vulnerable. If he didn't keep that secret to himself, I truly would lose everything. But I felt the need to invite someone to see my struggle. I had preached messages about finding healing when we bring our secrets into the light where we could be known. How it's our secrets that make us sick -- that only what is kept in darkness continues to have control over us.

"I don't know what to do," I said, pouring my heart out to him in a parking lot. "If my wife finds out, she will divorce me. Period. There's no coming back from that for us."

He kept this secret about me for roughly two years. Until one day, shortly after I had resigned as the Lead Pastor of our suburban megachurch, he shared everything he knew about me with my wife. I had never felt more betrayed than I did at that moment. I told myself that I would never trust anyone ever again. But then again, now that my deepest darkest secret was out — there wasn't anything else left to hide.

I can only imagine what was going on in my wife's mind when she was told this information. "Has our whole relationship been just one big charade?" I always thought that if there was some way to get her to enter into my own mind and heart — to think what I think and to feel what I feel — that everything would be different. But that's just impossible to do.

We tried to go back to couples counseling. But things were just never the same again. I felt as though she began to detach from me emotionally, and I knew that something had been severed that could never be reconnected.

As our marriage began to unravel in the coming months, the thought of not seeing my three children every day, putting them to bed at night, and waking up with them every morning, was more than I could bear. I was devastated.

By this time, I was working as Vice President of Advancement for a Christian missions organization. My wife was confiding about our marital struggles with many of her closest friends, so I had a feeling this news would spread to my new boss eventually. And it didn't take long. I showed up to work on a Monday morning, the day before my birthday, where I was met by the President, Vice President, and Director of Security of our organization. I was informed that I was fired from my job and my office had already been boxed up. I didn't blame them. They had to abide by their policies against homosexuality. And they certainly didn't need the drama that my failing marriage might bring.

In addition to severance, they did make a generous offer to me. They were willing to send me to a treatment facility in Arizona — but I would need to board a flight leaving later that morning. Oh, and I would be gone for 45 days! Leading up to this day, I was totally surrendered. I knew that my life was falling apart, and all I could do was trust God and hang on for the ride. Even though I wouldn't get the chance to say goodbye to my children, I agreed to go. I thought that it might be an excellent Christian reparative or conversion therapy program. Maybe this was what I had been missing all my life.

I was surprised to learn that it was actually a Sex Addiction Rehab Program. I didn't think I was a sex addict. In fact, I had always struggled with having a lower-than-normal libido.

"Do you think you're a sex addict?" asked the chief psychologist after looking over my initial test results. I was immediately afraid she would send me back home. There was something inside me that told me I needed to stay here. Something I needed to learn, know, and experience. I had hoped that maybe they could help me overcome my issue with same-sex attraction and that after 45 days of in-treatment programming, I'd finally be free. These were therapists that were not just the best in the nation — but the best in the world. Maybe this was my golden ticket.

I was temporarily disappointed when I realized that this place didn't do conversion therapy. They told me that it's now illegal in many states and that it doesn't work anyway. "If we did that to you, you would leave here more "effed up" than when you came in," was their response. What they would do for me though was to help me heal from everything I'd been through and help me to function, think, and live as a healthy, sexual individual – regardless of sexual orientation. For me, loving and accepting myself as a gay man was *not* an option — so it took me some time to even be open to that as a possibility.

I'll never forget my first-day meeting with my primary therapist, Bailey. As we sat down and talked about why I was there, I poured out my heart about what I had been carrying for so many years. I shared with her the absolute abhorrent disgust I had towards myself and my sexuality. The fact that there were some days I couldn't even stand to look at myself in the mirror. I confessed that I felt as if I had been the biggest disappointment to God and the church.

I'll never forget the question Bailey asked me. She said, "Brandon, if one of your three children came up to you and told you that they were gay… in light of all that you've been through and all you've experienced… how would you respond?"

My answer was easy. My eyes instantly filled with tears, and I replied, "I would give them the biggest hug, and I would never let go. I would tell them just how much I love them and how I feel their pain and their heartache and how I wish I could take it away from them. I would tell them that I love and accept them fully, just as they are. There was nothing I wanted for them more than for them to be who they are and to be happy."

Then Bailey said to me, "Brandon… if you as a Dad feel that way towards your own kids, how do you think your Heavenly Father wants to respond to you right now with this burden you've been carrying your whole life."

I sat there in silence for what seemed like an eternity. In that moment, it felt as if time stood still. I couldn't find any words to speak, so instead, I just sat there and wept. Tears started pouring down my cheeks as if a release valve had been opened up. Just as snow cannot resist the warmth of the sun, her statement began melting away something dark inside of me. Decades of shame and brokenness began to dissolve as I finally felt as if I could rest in the presence of a God who loved me unconditionally — just as I am.

Those 45 days in that inpatient program were some of the most defining moments of my life. It was the beginning of my "spiritual awakening," where I was introduced to meditation, mindfulness, and other ways of viewing spirituality from a holistic perspective. Everything I was now learning about spirituality felt congruent to my religious background -- yet more expansive, and it "just made perfect sense." For 45 days, I was growing in self-awareness, working through past trauma, learning about sexual orientation issues, and meeting with an entire team of therapists.

It was the best of times, yet it was also the worst of times. My wife filed for divorce shortly after I had arrived in Arizona for the treatment program. I'll never forget the day when Bailey, my primary therapist, told me we needed to have a conference call with my wife, myself, and a team of therapists. I thought nothing of it and just assumed it was a call about planning a visit for her to come out and see me. I was stunned to hear my wife say over the speakerphone that the reason for this call was to let me know that she had already filed for divorce and that the kids already knew. The conversation wasn't long. I was in too much of a shock to say much of anything. What was there left to say? I tried to stay strong and not break down into tears, but that strength failed quickly. Bailey could sense that my shock quickly transitioned to an emotional breakdown, so she promptly ended the call.

Looking back, I know that deep down, she was doing myself and her a favor. She knew there wasn't any hope in changing my sexual orientation. As angry as I was at first for being served divorce papers while still in rehab, I later considered it one of her last acts of love towards me. She wanted me to be surrounded 24/7 with people who could care for me when I found out that our marriage had ended.

Not once did I ever try to talk her out of the divorce in an effort to win her back. I knew I could never be the real husband to my wife that she longed for me to be. She would be better off without me. I felt immense shame for the hurt and wounds my life caused by not being honest about my truth. When you love people, you want what's best for them, and sometimes what's best for them isn't you. I knew I needed to let her go.

While I was there, two of my therapists had commented on separate occasions that it had been years since they had seen someone who had experienced more loss and heartache than I had. Another commented that when there was a Lifetime movie made about my life story, they wanted to be there for the premiere. This was certainly not the path to fame I was looking for.

> Each new chapter in our lives requests an old part of us to fall and a new part of us to rise.

As I checked out of rehab and was driven to Phoenix, where I would catch my flight back home, I reflected on how much my life had changed during that 45-day program. I was reminded of how the city of Phoenix was named after the immortal bird associated with Greek mythology. Even though the Phoenix would be burnt to the ground and seemingly destroyed, it would arise from the ashes in a newly resurrected form. The Phoenix felt like a metaphor for my life. The old Brandon had died in Arizona, and now I was leaving that old life behind me and moving on. Each new chapter of our lives requests an old part of us to fall and a new part of us to rise. Although I was looking forward to getting back and seeing my three kids, I dreaded coming back to Kansas City knowing what was ahead of me.

For 37 years, I thought I had done a pretty good job hiding my "secret" - but now that secret was out. Watching everything I'd accomplished crumble away almost overnight left me in a state of shock. My life felt like it was collapsing like an endless line of dominoes. The man that people perceived me to be ceased to exist. What was left? Was there anything worth living for?

At least I could be grateful that my life fell apart shortly after I had resigned as pastor of my church. I certainly didn't want to involve the church in my personal and family drama. However, I learned some rather disturbing news as I was returning home. Even though I had resigned months before, the megachurch that I loved and served for seven years had called a special business meeting with hundreds in attendance to inform them of the new developments that were going on in my life and in my failing marriage. Some church members wondered why leadership had pulled my past sermons from the church website and why my books were no longer sold in the bookstore. As it turns out, the church can be just as guilty of propagating "cancel culture" as much as the world is. Today, if a Christian leader has a failure, big or small, some people want to hold it over your head and believe that you no longer have a credible voice to help others. So, therefore, your life's work needs to be pulled from the shelves and wiped from existence. The decision for the church to "wipe every memory" of Brandon Park hurt immensely. It made me feel as though the body of Christ had turned its back on me permanently and completely. Church leadership had decided that answers regarding my personal life needed to be publicly given. Even though I hadn't been employed by the church for months, the meeting would satiate people's curiosity and allow them to "pray for my wife and me." So one Sunday night, hundreds of members gathered to hear a well-prepared statement regarding what was happening with me followed by a question and answer time. I was beyond shocked and appalled this meeting was allowed to have even taken place. I wasn't employed there anymore.

I had one attorney and a handful of angry church members encouraging me to file a lawsuit in response to this. But I had no desire to put myself or the church through any legal recourse. All I wanted was to be left alone to sort through the shattered pieces of my now broken life. Yet the aftermath of that church meeting was like pouring gasoline on a dumpster fire. The rumors that immediately spread about me were almost too much to bear. I became aware of six major rumors circulating about me that were so hideous, disgusting, and hurtful — two of which were even criminal in nature. I used to feel like my side of the story needed to be told to keep the facts right. By this point, I could care less what people chose to believe.

For a while, hardly a day went by that I didn't hear new gossip spreading about me. My biggest shame now seemed like the biggest talk of the town. My naked soul felt publicly humiliated as if I were shackled and displayed in the public square before a watching world.

One of my greatest fears was what my children would think of me. I love my kids so much I wouldn't think twice about giving up my life for them. But deep down, every father wants his children to be proud of him — at the very least, not be ashamed of him. My kids used to brag to their friends about what a great and successful man their father was. Now would they have anything left to brag about? Once they knew this about me, I feared I would lose their love and respect.

> "Depression is your avatar telling you it is tired of being the character you're trying to play."
> – Jim Carey

Depression was now like an old friend rather than a bothersome neighbor. I had struggled off and on with depression in the decade leading up to my divorce — even to the point of having to be medicated for it. I resonate with something Jim Carrey said: "Depression is your avatar telling you it is tired of being the character you're trying to play."

After being in the public eye and living in a glasshouse for the last two decades, I wanted nothing more than to silently disappear into the next chapter of my life. Nearly everyone I used to know had dropped all contact with me. Strangely, that didn't bother me as much as I initially thought it would. Every interaction with people I used to know highlighted, in my mind, that I was a disappointment to those who knew me. Starting a new life across the state line to the Kansas side of Kansas City seemed like my best option. That way, I could go to the grocery store without constantly running into people who knew me.

My parents had helped me move into my new apartment and stayed for a week to help me get settled. I knew that it would be hard to adjust to the new reality of living alone once they left. I said goodbye to my parents as they headed into their RV to make the long drive home. My Dad's parting words to me were: "You need to find a good church, pray that sinners prayer again, and get baptized." I didn't know how to respond to that. I felt shocked and confused. It brought me back to those memories of being a young, insecure child who had prayed and begged God to save me so many times. I had been following Jesus for 26 years. I had preached the gospel for nearly 20 years and led thousands to follow Christ as well. None of that mattered anymore. My own father apparently thought I was lost.

After Mom and Dad left, I just sat in my chair for the longest time and cried. Reality had set in that this is now how many would perceive me. If my own father was capable of thinking I was lost and in need to be saved, how many more would think that? It didn't matter that I had a genuine personal relationship with God or knew the gospel well enough to lead thousands to faith in Christ during my two decades in ministry. In the eyes of many Christians, the presence of homosexuality automatically means you must be lost and in need of salvation yourself. The same father who once beamed with pride over his son's accomplishments and would lavish me with praise after every sermon I would preach — now believed that his favored son was lost and in need of salvation. It reminded me of how I felt as a teenager of never feeling like God accepted me because I had this attraction. I feared that maybe I didn't cry out to God hard enough for salvation because the gay never went away. If only my father knew that one of the primary reasons I went into ministry — the very thing he was so proud of me for — was partially because I was trying to overcompensate for this shame I already felt.

Not long after, two other former church members attempted to "evangelize" me on Facebook. Soon, another church member reached out to me by phone. I was quickly made aware of his actual intentions. He asked point blank, "Brandon, have you ever accepted Jesus Christ into your heart and life to be your Lord and Savior?" This question felt insulting and presumptuous. I felt a mixture of confusion, anger, and disgust at his question. It also felt more like an attack, a twisting-of-the-knife, than a genuine concern for my soul. I don't remember everything I said in my response to him, but I'm sure it wasn't gracious. Here was a man making assumptions about my own salvation when my relationship with God was literally the only thing I had left to hold onto. My faith was the only thing keeping me alive at that moment -- it was the only thing that was still sacred and immutable. And now, I felt aggravated and revolted that even that was being called into question. Unfortunately, I started allowing the assumptions of others about my salvation to push me further away from God and not closer to Him. Being on the receiving end of that evangelistic or "soul-winning" question made me also wonder how many people I had inadvertently pushed away from God in an effort to "win them to Jesus."

For a brief time, God felt more distant than ever. Even though I felt a great deal of personal responsibility, I was also angry at Him for allowing me to be in this situation. My entire life had been planned around a career in ministry for God. I had thrown my heart and soul into doing everything I thought God had asked me to do in order to become straight — and I felt like He didn't keep His end of the deal. God seemed to disappear from the chaos that had become my life. The armor of perfection I had worn every day wasn't just cracking. It was crumbling. The humiliation of my failures screamed for attention.

On one particular Saturday night in December, I received a message from yet another former church member that was so hurtful and full of these allegations that I felt like I could never recover from this. In that message, she had conveyed that she had heard the rumor (a new one to me) that I might be suspected of being a child pedophile (because apparently, if you struggle with same-sex attraction, it must automatically make you want to abuse little boys). My initial shock and outrage quickly morphed into utter despair. I really thought that things couldn't get any worse after all I had already experienced. I had never experienced more anguish and more pain than I did that night. I had never felt more alone, abandoned, betrayed than I did in that moment. That was the tipping point for me. I was done. I believed that if people I loved and served for years could think that I would even be capable of doing something like that, I no longer had any reason left to live. I was better off dead. So I had resolved in my mind that the best thing for me to do moving forward was to make a plan to end my life.

I began contemplating how to put an end to the pain. I would drive around town just sobbing uncontrollably. My car seemed to be the only place where I could feel safe to mourn the loss of everything I knew up to that point. I needed a safe place to grieve where I wouldn't cause a scene. I would drive to an abandoned parking lot where no one was around and would scream at the top of my lungs through the tears. It was part venting to God how I was feeling and part yelling at God for the situation I found myself in. Those screaming and crying fits became a regular practice. I was releasing decades of pent-up emotion and pain.

I had lost my entire support system. I'd been erased from my church, and was now estranged from all my friends. One by one, I watched as all of the supporters that were donating to my non-profit ministry drop off. Within 6 months after my divorce, I had lost all of my financial partners, except for my parents and three others. As a result, I had to close down the non-profit organization I had founded after leaving my pastoral career.

I felt deserted by my former supporters. I never heard from them again. But then again, I didn't blame them. I felt abandoned by my "friends" as well, but I didn't fault them for it under the circumstances. One of my former friends confessed that he needed to distance himself from me because he feared that any association with me meant that people might doubt his sexuality too. How could I blame him for wanting to cut me off? I was poison. It was in his best interests to do so. I had already decided to make it easier on everyone by distancing myself from all who had previously known me. It would just be better for everyone that way.

I used to be a megachurch pastor. But now I felt an inordinate amount of shame over what I used to do in my previous career. For 19 years, I had preached hope, but I now felt utterly hopeless.

I was forced to look for another line of work. I was unemployable both to the church I had devoted my life to as well as to the business world. No church would have me speak. I had trained and built for my entire life a career in ministry, but now that career was entirely over. In addition to my own living expenses of rent and utilities, I now had the legal obligation to pay monthly child support and alimony payments with absolutely no income coming in. Fortunately, I did qualify for food stamps, so at least I was able to eat and feed my kids. But my job search was terribly demoralizing. No one wanted to hire me. "How am I going to make it?" I asked. "What business is going to hire a guy who was a preacher for the last 20 years?" I have four degrees from seminary that are utterly useless outside the church world. I felt completely unmarketable for employment. And because I had worked for non-profits, I was ineligible for unemployment benefits.

With each passing day, I was simultaneously drawn to suicide and found myself fantasizing about while also sensing the responsibility to stay and raise my children. They were all that I had left worth living for. I used to think that a person who is suicidal was being selfish and not thinking about those he would leave behind. That they were only thinking of themselves and not the pain that would be left in the wake of their passing. But in those moments of reaching your lowest point - you truly (yet falsely) believe that the most loving thing you can do for your loved ones is to remove your life from existence. I was believing the lie that it was in the best interests of my own children not to have me as their father.

There's an Arabic saying that goes: "You want to die? Then throw yourself into the sea, and you'll see yourself fighting to survive. You do not want to kill yourself. Rather, you want to kill something inside of you." There's much truth to that. I wanted to live, but at that moment, I could only see my future looking worse, not better.

The turning point for me happened one cold winter morning. I was at Starbucks working on my exit plan and getting my affairs in order. I was writing instructions for my parents on where to find stuff, passwords for my bank accounts, retirement and stock accounts, etc. I knew that my death would be brutal for them, so I wanted to eliminate as much stress as possible by having everything neatly organized. I worried about how many days it would take before someone actually knew I was dead. I was living like a hermit with little contact with anyone by this point. Would my body be partially decomposed by the time someone found me? Would that be too traumatic for them to witness that? What could I do to mitigate that so my body wouldn't be left

Those were the thoughts ruminating through my mind as I began to write my suicide note to loved ones.

alone to rot in that apartment all by itself? Those were the thoughts ruminating through my mind as I began to write my suicide note to loved ones. I had chosen a table at Starbucks where my face was pointed to the corner so that no one could see my tears. Typing that suicide letter caused those tears to quickly turn to sobs, and I knew I needed to leave before someone could see me.

As I headed to my car, I felt so scared because it really did feel like this was something I would go through with. So many dominoes of suicidal ideation had been tipped by that time, and it seemed as though a wave of momentum was pulling me in that direction. I wondered if I needed to check myself into a mental hospital. But then again, I had no insurance, so how would I pay for that if I did later find the will to live? As I got into my car, the thought occurred to me, "Maybe I need to call a hotline and talk to somebody?" I remembered hearing about the National Suicide Prevention Hotline, so I googled the number. I just needed to hear another person's voice who would understand. Still, I didn't want to call my parents or a family member because I knew they would worry and would immediately be driving out to Kansas City to be with me. I didn't want to put them through that burden.

I sat in the car in silence, mustering up enough courage to finally take that first step to make the phone call to that hotline. I dialed the number and expected to hear another human voice on the other end of the line. Instead, it was an automated voice message: "Thank you for calling the National Suicide Prevention hotline. If you're a veteran, dial 1 now, to speak with someone, dial 2 now…" For whatever reason, I found so much humor in this. My sobs and tears quickly turned to a chuckle as I could only imagine someone standing on the edge of a bridge ready to jump but then calling that hotline as one last effort to live. I think if I were standing on a bridge, getting a lifelessly robotic and automated message would have definitely pushed me over. "You've got to be kidding me," I said to myself. I found some humor in the irony of the situation. The thought occurred to me: "Maybe I need to live just a little bit longer so I can fix this situation. Someone needs to immediately hear a real human voice when they call a suicide prevention number."

Out of nowhere, I felt as if this powerful thought was downloaded into my spirit: "This is who you are. You're created to fix broken things and heal broken people. You have many more assignments to influence others and be a beacon light. Your best days are still ahead of you." That impression came out of nowhere. It wasn't the audible voice of God, but it felt so powerful, abrupt, and profound that I immediately knew it had to come from Spirit. My name "Brandon" means "beacon of light." God wanted me to know that my time was nowhere near over. I still had work to do.

I'm not sure what happened to me that day, but it was a transformative moment. After that, I never again entertained any thought of suicide. It was as if one chapter in my life had ended, and now another was beginning. I genuinely believe that every single person has to go through something that absolutely destroys them in order for them to figure out who they really are. As Robin Williams said, "A hungry stomach, an empty wallet, and a broken heart can teach you the best lessons of life." Sometimes from the bitterest experience comes the greatest awakening. When we hit our lowest point, only then are we are open for the greatest change.

> I genuinely believe that every person has to go through something that absolutely destroys them in order for them to figure out who they really are.

Sometimes the most painful thing you will ever have to let go of is an older version of yourself. Yet to wholeheartedly embrace the authentic you is liberating, freeing, and life-changing. It's what causes people to be drawn to you like a magnet because your authenticity enriches and refreshes their lives when they're around you. When I considered all of the beautiful experiences and success I had over my lifespan, I'd been living with the belief that the best years of my life were behind me. But now, for the first time, I was seeing that what lay ahead for me in this new chapter was a future brighter than anything I'd previously imagined.

I began praying that God would send people to me to help me understand and make sense of everything I was sorting through. Then, one by one, God began answering that prayer and sending specific individuals to cross my path. He started placing people along my way that showed me what I needed to see about myself and the nature of reality.

I remember asking one of these new acquaintances, "How can you believe the Bible *and* accept homosexuality?" My understanding of pro-gay theology up to that point was that it was only used to justify sin. Liberal or progressive Christians weren't really genuine Christians anyway. How could they be if they didn't believe in the inerrancy and infallibility of Scripture?

> A faith that cannot be questioned cannot be trusted.

"Just because we don't interpret the Bible the way you do doesn't mean we don't accept it to be God's inspired Word," this friend said. "We just see it differently." The fact that they still believed in the inspiration of Scripture without necessarily holding to the inerrancy of Scripture made me think I could meet them halfway and actually listen to their perspective.

I started asking honest questions. Are there interpretations of the Bible, other than the ones I was raised to believe and reinforced in seminary that make sense? What is it about the Bible that skeptics have such issues and disagreements with? Could there be another interpretation of the passages that seem to condemn homosexuality? It was the first time in my conservative/evangelical/fundamentalist life that I dared to look at things with fresh eyes. Before, I was literally afraid to view other perspectives or interpretations because I was terrified that my faith would come tumbling down like a house of cards if I did. And I couldn't risk that. I had staked my livelihood on being in full-time ministry. Having doubt in my belief system would inevitably cause significant distress and potentially a loss of employment. Now I found myself in a different place. I now had the opportunity to look at things differently without the risk of losing my job. I began praying that God would reveal truth to me and keep me from error each day. I was deeply afraid that I would entirely fall away from my faith by questioning my long-held beliefs. But a faith that cannot be questioned cannot be trusted. Instead, the exact opposite happened. My faith became refortified; my spirituality was more potent than it had ever been before.

Years ago, I remember seeing a video pop up on my social media newsfeed of four soldiers driving a military jeep in a parade. All four of them got out of the vehicle and proceeded to completely take it apart, piece by piece, down to the wheels, the chassis, and even the engine — and then reassemble and put it all back together again — all within a matter of minutes. It was fascinating to watch their well-timed coordination and precision in completely dismantling and then reassembling a vehicle in such a short amount of time. In many ways, I feel like that's an analogy of what happened to me in my faith journey. I found that my deconstruction of not just my faith but who I understood myself to be was a grueling process that took place part-by-part, piece-by-piece. But by the grace of God, I feel like I've slowly been put back together (with a few much-needed tune-ups, so I'm now running better than I was before). And the result is that my view of God and my love for Him has grown expansively. I'm experiencing direct and unmistakable answers to prayer on a level as I've never experienced before. The parts of the Bible that were difficult to accept or seemed contradictory now made total sense within their proper place of this interpretive framework.

I never really "came out" of the closet. I was kicked out. I sometimes jokingly say that I was so far deep in the closet, I was in Narnia! I had resolved to live my life in denial of who I was. As painful as it was being publicly exposed, I now see it as a gift because of what it taught me through this process. And I also have a lot more respect for those who do come out of the closet out of their own free will and acknowledge to their loved ones, "This is who I am."

> "Religion is one of the safest places to hide from God."
> - Richard Rohr

Richard Rohr used to say, "Religion is one of the safest places to hide from God." I feel that. Rather than fully resting in my connection and oneness with God, I used to find refuge in my performance for Him.

Even though I've come to a deep acceptance of who I am and am fully resting in my walk with God, I still struggle with external influences regarding my sexual orientation. I fight the shame and disappointment that my family has to incur because of who I am. I hate knowing that I have let my parents and relatives down because I did not fulfill their image of my ideal life. I hate how the good in my life and the past works I've done are now so often seen as invalid because of this. Even though I've fully healed from internal shame, I still sense the projected shame of others and society at large. With every passing day, though, I grow more at peace and confident with myself that I don't absorb that negative energy surrounding me.

There is nothing more exhausting than living an inauthentic life. Our sexual identity is as integral to who we are as our religious upbringings are. To separate these aspects of ourselves — to separate life as a sexual being from a life with God — is to bifurcate our psyche. And for the first time in my life, I feel like I'm living congruently — where my spirituality, religiosity, and sexuality — all come together in harmony. Like the Phoenix, what had almost destroyed me had actually developed me. What was left in those ashes was my shame, pain, misunderstandings, and inauthenticity. What rose up out of those ashes was a version of me unrecognizable to my former self -- a soul that had been healed. For the first time in my life, I could look in the mirror and love the person I was becoming. And most importantly, I knew that God loved me too.

WALK A MILE IN MY SHOES

""Walk a day in my shoes, feel the pain, loss, sadness, guilt, remorse, and the heartache, then I dare you to judge me."
- Anonymous

It's the old adage: Before you judge someone, walk a mile in his shoes. To truly love and understand someone, you need to be able to experience life as they do. As Toni Sorenson once said, "Walking a mile in someone else's shoes isn't as much about the walk or the shoes; it's to be able to think as they think, feel what they feel, and understand why they are who they are and where they are. Every step is about empathy." Empathy is the capacity to think and feel oneself into the inner life of another person. It's the ability of seeing with the eyes of another, listening with the ears of another, and feeling with the heart of another. That's why the highest form of knowledge is empathy. That's why Mohsin Hamid said, "Empathy is about finding echoes of another person in yourself."

Every gay man or lesbian woman you will ever meet has fought a lifelong battle about which you likely know little or nothing. And if you're reading this as a person within the LGBTQ community, you need this chapter because having insight into childhood experiences creates changes in adult behavior. Understanding the factors that molded and shaped who you are today will likely answer many questions. The key to thriving as a human being — straight or gay — is having a profound sense of self-awareness.

Since our culture today is so good at stereotyping, here are ten common traits about LGBTQ individuals. I'm writing this as a gay man. Still, I feel that many of these characteristics are replicated across the entire spectrum of the queer community. The thing about generalizations is that they are generally true, yet they may not apply to every individual. Here are ten little-known facts about your gay loved ones that will allow you to enter their hearts and minds and proverbially "walk in their shoes" to gain greater clarity and understanding as to how they think and how their view of the world was shaped by the non-affirming culture surrounding them.[1]

1. Shame can be our core emotion and the root of our identity.

Many of my coaching clients have suppressed this shame so much that they don't even feel it until it's uncovered in the deeper work of therapy. Shame is not the same as homophobia. Homophobia is the fear of being gay; shame is the fear of being unlovable. Homophobia may go away over time, but the shame will last a lifetime unless it's dealt with. Gay shame is not embarrassment over being gay. It is the belief that being gay is a mere symptom of being overtly flawed. It is within this experience of "differentness" — not being like your peers, not being the one who fits in — that shame takes root in our lives.

The wound that all gay men have is the trauma caused by exposure to overwhelming shame at an age when you weren't equipped to cope with it. Because we are so vulnerable to shame and it's so easily triggered within us, our lives become solely focused on avoiding shame and seeking validation.

Shame is not the same thing as guilt. As the well-known shame researcher and writer Brene Brown explains:

Guilt = I did something bad.

Shame = I am bad.

When you are taught that being gay is "bad," and you cannot change that aspect of your nature, you assume that you are also bad at the very core of your being. Shame goes far deeper, and it's infinitely more painful than guilt. Brene Brown's definition of shame is "the fear of disconnection." It's the fear of being unlovable. It's the belief that you are flawed and therefore unworthy of belonging. And LGBTQ people risk this pain of rejection perhaps more than any other demographic today.

> Shame is the belief that you are flawed and therefore unworthy of belonging.

Dr. David Hawkins demonstrates some of the most potent research about human emotion I've ever come across. In his book *Power vs. Force: The Hidden Determinants of Human Behavior*, he discovered that the human body emits an energetic frequency that can be either positive, neutral, or negative, depending on what emotions we are feeling at any given time. His research showed how a simple muscle test revealed that negative emotions weaken the muscle (and therefore the entire body) and positive emotions strengthen it. He delineated these different emotions on a scale (peace, joy, love demonstrating the highest emotional frequencies while negative emotions of anger, fear, grief, apathy, and guilt were associated with the lowest or weakest frequencies). When we consistently live with the most negative emotions, we actually invite not only poorer relationships and emotional health; but we also position our body to be more prone to sickness, disease, and even cancer. And guess what emotion is at the bottom of Hawkins's scale? The absolute most detrimental negative emotion we can experience in this lifetime is not anger, sadness or guilt. *It is shame.*

Gay men are unconsciously taught to live in secrecy from a very young age. That secrecy bleeds over into shame around relationships. Substance abuse and/or alcohol is one of the ways many men learn to avoid shame. If we could get high enough for long enough, we could forget the disgrace that dogs us throughout the day. Only then could we let go and have a good time. Another way that most gay men avoid shame is through anonymous sex. It's quick, easy, no ties, no names. After all, if you don't know his name, you have a great excuse never to call or talk to him again. When you're known intimately, you risk your flaws and shortcomings being made known. It's within those anonymous encounters that gay men receive a temporarily fleeting moment of validation. However, using anonymous sex to compensate for the internalized shame we feel is like drinking ocean saltwater to quench our thirst. It never leaves a person feeling fulfilled.

Almost everything gay men do becomes an avoidance strategy or an invitation for validation. Avoiding shame becomes the single most powerful driving force in his life. Did you know that nothing can destroy iron, but its own rust can? So likewise, nothing can ruin a person, but his own shame can. This is why your gay loved one needs you. Brene Brown says, "If we share our story with someone who responds with empathy and understanding, shame can't survive." This is why empathy is like a universal solvent. Any problem immersed in empathy becomes soluble.

2. We are desperate for love and validation.

We seek validation every day. It's one of the most essential psychological needs of every person. And yet, many gay men and women don't receive that validation from the peers and family members they love and crave it from the most. As British psychiatrist R.D. Laing noted: "Whether life is worth living depends on whether there is love in life." This early, crippling shame taught us that if you are to be loved, you must hide the truth about yourself and work hard in order to be lovable. As a result, many gay men have an experience of going through a stage where they take on many sexual partners to try to make themselves feel attractive, sexy, and lovable — all in an attempt to avert shame and gain validation.

As we matured with this growing knowledge of being different — there was an equally expanding fear that our "differentness" would cause us to lose the love and affection of our parents. One day in middle school, I remember my Dad waiting with me in the car at the school bus stop. And he asked me, "Brandon, do you like girls?" I knew I was supposed to, and of course, I said yes. But I also knew the motive for my father asking that question. He hadn't seen any evidence of that fact. My perceived fear of losing my father's love, acceptance, and approval was too great of a risk to take. I had also hoped at that age, that when I did meet the right girl, then the right desires would be awakened in me.

Later in adolescence, this anxiety developed into a fear of rejection by classmates. The playground is likely the first place that most gay men realized they were different from the other boys. We didn't necessarily want to play the same games. We weren't as athletic or aggressive as them, yet we feared being taunted or teased because we didn't fit in.

Dale from Charleston, North Carolina, said,

I can't remember when it started, but I can definitely remember always feeling like I didn't fit in. I can remember sitting alone on the playground even when I was in kindergarten. I didn't want to do all the stupid things the other boys were doing, like sword fighting with sticks or playing cowboys and Indians. Even back then, it all seemed so strange to me.

So many LGBTQ children feel alone. I felt alone. Even though I knew I had parents that loved me and wanted the absolute best for me, I was fearful that if they knew me as I knew me — that things would be different. Like most families growing up in the '80s and 90s, we chose awkward silence over awkward conversations. Children want nothing more than for their parents to not just love them but to be proud of them for who they are. They want their father's approval and their mother's unconditional love. Unfortunately, this solitary issue of sexuality becomes the one factor that rips many of my gay friends' families apart.

> How can we love ourselves when everything around us tells us that we are unlovable?

How can we love ourselves when everything around us tells us that we are unlovable? So instead, we chased the affection, approval, and attention doled out by others. In my experience, I found this from the people that I had pastored. Their approval of me was like a drug, and I was an addict to the love, praise, and adoration they would express towards me. This drove me to become a workaholic — where I would spend 70 to 80 hours a week as a pastor. I needed my following message to be another "home-run" so I wouldn't lose what I felt was the only source of love and acceptance for who I am and what I did.

The little boy with the dark secret becomes the man driven to avoid shame by hiding who he is. He develops a sophisticated radar for those things and people who will make him feel good about himself.

3. We will overcompensate for our feelings of inadequacy.

It might surprise you to discover that many of the wealthiest and most successful men in society today are gay men. Others grow up with a keen sense of culture, fashion, or interior design. Many others are devoted to making sure their Adonis body is in peak condition by spending countless hours in the gym. He attempts to become "hyper-masculine" by working out all the time or by becoming a star athlete so that no one suspects the real truth about him. Many will spend all their spare time at the gym, building what they believe is the body that will one day earn them enough adoration to satisfy their craving for it. Their struggles with body dysmorphia are real, and aging is seen as one of the worst things we can experience in life. In our minds, to age is to become less desirable. Therefore getting regular Botox injections and facials is of paramount importance. They are fabulous and outrageous hosts for parties and events. They're an arbiter of good taste and elegant design. They are pop-culture aficionados.

No one knows how to create style more than gay men. Gay men are worldwide experts on style, fashion, etiquette, bodybuilding, art, and design. There are even hit television shows about it — *Queer Eye for the Straight Guy*. We decorate our lives. We decorate our bodies. We decorate the world — all in an effort to hide our real selves from society.

Something about the experience of being gay causes us to develop our "fashion skills." We specialize in makeovers of all types and sizes. We're experts in making people, things, and ourselves look good. Growing up gay forced us to learn how to hide ugly

> Growing up gay forced us to learn how to hide ugly realities behind a finely crafted façade.

realities behind a finely crafted facade. Why is this so? Because we realized that hiding is a means to survival. The naked truth about who we are wasn't acceptable to society, so we learned to cope by hiding behind a beautiful image. We compartmentalized ourselves by hiding what wasn't acceptable and flaunting what was.

But when you peel away these well-crafted layers, only then can you see their deepest secret clearly for what it is. Their deepest secret is not having a sexual orientation towards the same sex. It's something far darker and disastrous. It's his own self-hatred.

4. Many of us have "daddy issues."

As a boy, the first man you loved was your father, and you craved from him love, affection, and tenderness. Unfortunately, what most of us received from our fathers fell very short. The tenderness we needed was replaced with spanking and/or harshly chastising us whenever we did something wrong. Corporal punishment, such as spanking, affected gay boys much differently than other boys. We internalized it more.

One gay man in Miami once told me, "I so desperately wanted and needed that love and affection from my father. I believe that partially, one of the reasons I'm gay today is because I'm still trying to receive through the arms of other men what I never received from my own father." It was common for fathers of previous generations to be taught to be tough, stable, and emotionally detached by their own dads.

Whatever the cause of our "daddy issues," most of us grew into our young adulthoods without ever having had a truly loving, honest, and safe relationship with another man, not with our buddies, and not with our fathers. In the course of psychotherapy, more than a few gay men have been amazed to realize how close many of their ex-lovers' personality characteristics were similar to their father's.

Suppose their dad was emotionally withdrawn, judgmental, or physically abusive. In that case, they are shocked to discover that former lovers were cut from the same fabric. For many gay men, their father is the only model they have of a close male relationship — so when they see their father in another man who validates them and finds them attractive — they marry him. We take refuge in what's familiar and safe.

Tom, from Seattle, Washington, said,

> I never spoke with my father about my being gay. Years ago, I told my mother, and, of course, I knew she'd tell my dad. I know that he knew, but we never talked about it. I just couldn't bear to see the disappointment on his face. Now that he's gone, I grieve for him — and for us — when I think about it because we never were able to be friends. Friends? Hell, we weren't even able to talk.

This is by far the most damaging of all of the invalidation that gay men receive in their lives. The first man that we love — arguably the man we will love the most in our life — is incapable of validating us at a time when we need it the most. That wound will affect most of us through the rest of our lives.

Our mother, too — likely realized we were different. Many moms move in to protect us from what they rightly sensed would be our fathers' slow, subtle, and unconscious betrayal. As a result, she nurtured us, favored us, and over-validated us to compensate for the betrayal she saw us suffer. As a result of this over-compensating protection we felt from our mothers, many of us developed more feminine qualities, which resulted in a better-developed tender side. We cultivated creative, compassionate, and nurturing talents.

5. Gay men often feel more comfortable in the company of women.

Gay men are often the best friends a woman can find. With a gay man, there are no taboo subjects or fear of being misunderstood. And women feel safer to be themselves — knowing she isn't being targeted or wooed. Even better than this, this man and woman are not competing for the same men! Gay men also have no qualms about their feminine side as opposed to straight men who feel the need to act rigidly macho.

There's actually a physiological reason for this. PET and MRI studies performed in 2008 have shown that the two halves of the brain are more symmetrical in homosexual men and heterosexual women than in heterosexual men and homosexual women. These studies have also revealed that connections in the amygdala of gay men resemble those of straight women; in gay women, connections in the amygdala resemble those of straight men. The amygdala has many receptors for sex hormones and is associated with the processing of emotions.[1]

6. Gay men usually have an increased ability to feel people's emotions around them.

Those who feel the most misunderstood in their childhood desire to bring the most empathy, healing, and understanding to others in their adulthood.

They are usually more intuitive. Their emotional intelligence usually ranks higher than their straight counterparts. It's very common for gay men to go into service-type roles with their careers. They are today's counselors, psychologists, social workers, worship leaders, and yes... even pastors. Why? Sometimes, those who feel the most misunderstood in their childhood desire to bring the most empathy, healing, and understanding to others in their adulthood. Because growing up in the closet means that you were probably known as "the fixer." So it's easier to focus on others and fix their problems. I don't know how many times I've heard the words, "You're so easy to talk to" or "I feel like I could tell you anything." But many times, the reason people are so good at being there for others is because, deep down, they desperately need someone to be like that for them. And if you're not careful, life will pass you by because you were busy being everything to everyone but yourself. In the years I spent listening to everyone else, I never felt like I trusted anyone enough to open up about me. And they never asked... because they all think that you're a rock. But to me, I was a mess. I knew I was different — and I didn't want to be. No one ever knew the secret struggle I was going through.

7. Gay individuals will go through three distinct life stages.

And each of these stages deals primarily with how we have learned to navigate our primary emotion in adolescence: "shame."

The first stage is **"Crippled by Shame."** This is when the gay man or lesbian woman is "in the closet" and fearful of their own sexuality and fearful of not being accepted by family, peers, and society. He would do anything not to be gay. He suffers immensely from the pain of knowing that he can't change the one thing that makes him so different from others. He imagines that being gay will ruin his life completely, and...there is nothing he can do to stop it. No amount of dating girls, playing straight and wishing or praying to God to change it takes it away. He is faced with the debilitating and crippling reality that he is irreversibly queer. The most common way gay men seek to avoid shame is to deny their sexuality. For many, the most challenging part about coming out is really

> For many, the most challenging part about coming out is really just coming out to yourself.

51

just coming out to yourself. We simply acted as if we weren't gay. After all, our logic went, if we didn't act gay, maybe we weren't.

I distanced myself from a dear friend that others perceived as quite obviously gay in high school. It seemed to me at the time that if I was seen with him, others would see the similarities between us and discover my secret too. Along with many of my coaching clients, I married a woman in what I can now see as a desperate attempt to deny my true sexuality. Many gay men still living in denial will gravitate towards strong, anti-gay activities and organizations. As I've mentioned previously, intense homophobia is one of the most significant indicators of repressed homosexuality. As the German poet Herman Hesse brilliantly said, "If you hate a person, you hate something in him that is part of yourself. What isn't part of ourselves doesn't disturb us."

The second stage is **"Compensating for Shame,"** and this describes the gay man's attempt to neutralize his shame by being more successful, outrageous, fabulous, beautiful, or masculine. We try to make ourselves more acceptable to others in various ways. Perhaps by displaying creativity that other boys refused to show or winning the approval of teachers and other adults by excelling at everything we did. For me personally, I over-compensated by trying to wear the nicest clothes I could afford (spending ridiculous amounts of money on Abercrombie and Fitch as a teen), by being an over-achiever making straight A's to outshine all my peers (I eventually graduated valedictorian at my Christian school), and going into the ministry as a pastor. Being a Lead Pastor made me feel validated by my family, my church, and most importantly… my understanding of God at that time. Unfortunately, many queer individuals will always remain stuck in this second stage. Until a gay man is willing to reexamine his life, he will likely remain blind to the root of shame that continues to cripple his life.

However, some heal enough to make it to the third stage, **"Cultivating Authenticity."** Once they reach this stage, they can build a life based on their own passions and values rather than subconsciously proving to themselves and others that they are desirable and lovable. Gay men and women that go through the necessary deep work to get to this stage are truly the models of authenticity and courage and the cleansers of shame.

Sadly, it took me nearly 40 years to get to this point. When you understand what a momentous breakthrough this is for gay men to reach this point — you begin to empathize and understand why "coming out" is such a big deal. The reason why the gay community is known for gay pride parades and "National Coming Out Days" isn't because they are trying to flaunt their sexuality in front of straight people. It's because, for them, the ability to come out of the closet and live authentically — knowing the damning ramifications of that decision — is perhaps the most courageous act they've ever done. Once that glass ceiling has been broken — they finally have a desire to live "out and proud." The reason why straight people don't understand Gay Pride is because they have never had to live with gay shame and secrecy. Heterosexual people have never had to hide their sexual orientation or fear the reactions of others

> The reason why straight people don't understand "Gay Pride" is because they have never had to live with gay shame and secrecy.

for being who they are. They'll never have to hide their heterosexuality in order to be accepted or walk down the street and have someone yell hurtful words at them because they are straight. They are always perceived as "normal." When you hear of Gay Pride, remember that it was not born out of a need to celebrate being gay. It evolved out of our need as human beings to break free of oppression and to exist without being criminalized, pathologized, or persecuted. Instead of wondering why there isn't a straight pride parade, just be grateful that you never needed one.

Whoever came up with the concept of "Pride" when naming gay Pride Marches or Pride Month was definitely clever. Because what is the very opposite of pride? Shame. Contrary to what many evangelicals have accused the gay community of doing, they're not trying to shove their lifestyle onto others or parade their sexuality around to a watching world. Instead, they merely celebrate a breakthrough of overcoming the shame that was years, perhaps even decades in the making.

8. We develop a pseudo-self.

When LGBTQ people are in the closet, they feel as if they are living someone else's life. As a result of living in stage two — "Compensating for Shame," we became adept at playing the part that family, church, and society expect from us. It was a self that would earn us validation by others, while our true selves remained hidden from everyone. Many of us play the part by participating in sports so we can be included with the other boys or by taking a girl to prom so we'd fit in — all while knowing it was a farce.

The only type of validation that really counts and matters to anyone is authentic validation. When you're living under false pretenses, and you're complimented on that — it's a nice gesture, but it feels hollow and shallow. It would be like driving your neighbor's new sports car convertible and receiving compliments on it. It's nice to hear, but you don't feel validated by it since it really isn't your car. Authentic validation is honest validation of something that matters to you. This is the plight of every gay man who is still living in the closet. Any validation we receive while in that state is hollow, baseless, and not satisfying. We're living someone else's life. The young gay boy who learns to "fake out" everyone and act straight becomes starved for authentic validation. And without the inoculating effects of authentic validation, shame is debilitating. It causes us to withdraw and want to hide.

Alexander Leon perhaps framed this struggle best when he said, "Queer people don't grow up as ourselves. We grow up playing a version of ourselves that sacrifices authenticity to minimize humiliation and prejudice. The massive task of our adult lives is to unpick which parts of ourselves are truly us and which parts we've created to protect us."

9. We have suppressed anger issues that stem from this.

Sometimes that anger is directed at parents, siblings, a partner, the church, or even God. Repressed shame and an inability to satisfy your own needs is a deadly combination. Feelings of rage begin to emerge. When the unhealed gay man is not living authentically, his tolerance for invalidation becomes dangerously low, and his hunger for validation becomes all-consuming.

As Alan Downs writes in his book, Velvet Rage:

> Rage is the experience of intense anger that results from his failing to achieve authentic validation. Since authentic validation can occur only in the context of one's true, authentic self, he finds himself incapable of achieving the one thing that will bring him lasting contentment. Like a cornered and terrified animal, he is provoked and terrified animal, he is provoked, snarling and demanding that he be set free from the cage to which he has been leashed. Of course, his rage only pushes others away, and the sacred validation that he craves goes with them. So he hides his anger in the velvet glove, quickly returning to the gracious friend and lover he aspires to be. Life, then, becomes an ever vacillating seesaw between rage and gentility. He reaches out to his world for validation, always sensitive to the slightest invalidation, to which he responds with swift rage.

Gay men tend to overreact. Whenever their shame and hypersensitivity to invalidation seem triggered, they feel them with an intensity beyond what the circumstance merits. As a result, gay men have often been known to become furious over the most minor issue. It's been referred to as the "crash and lash syndrome" — a verbal slight, an off-hand insult, a disapproving look — any of those factors have been known to trigger the crash and lash syndrome of rage. Sometimes people who need the most love act out in unloving ways.

As a result, there's often a cynical attitude among gay men regarding finding real love and the possibility of longevity in a gay relationship. Many of my friends have shared previous experiences of falling in love then being hurt or betrayed, which hardened them. Subsequently, every time they met someone new, they immediately sabotaged the relationship, deciding it was only a matter of time before that person would prove false. Predictably, they always get what they expected, the self-fulfilling prophecy always coming to pass.

> Anything that triggers us is a window to the unhealed parts of our being.

Perhaps Eckhart Tolle worded it best: "Where there is anger, there is always pain underneath." Anger is simply the outward manifestation of deep inner wounds. One of the best definitions of anger I've ever heard was this: "It's the punishment we give to ourselves for somebody else's mistake." Anything that triggers us is a window to the unhealed parts of our being. If you don't heal what hurt you, you will bleed on people who didn't cut you. When you finally learn that a person's behavior has more to do with their own internal struggle than it ever did with you… you learn grace.

10. We are more likely to contemplate suicide.

Chances are, your loved one who is gay has considered or even attempted it. One of the most drastic measures that gay men resort to in order to avoid experiencing the toxic shame of being gay is by ending their lives. Suicide among gay men (especially in stage one) is shockingly common. One study found that homosexual males (whether out or not) account for more than half of all male youth suicide attempts. Another study of gay and bisexual males age fifteen to twenty-six found that 54 percent of them had seriously considered suicide compared to only 13 percent of men in the general population. The sad reality for many gay men is that their overwhelming shame feels mortally unbearable.

Harper Lee, in the legendary book To Kill a Mockingbird, writes: "You never really understand a person until you consider things from his point of view...until you climb into his skin and walk around in it." When you put yourself into your gay loved one's shoes, you realize — if it hurts you, it probably hurts them too. We develop empathy when we realize that every person we meet, reacting to every decision they will ever make — that individual is doing the very best they can according to their current level of consciousness. If Christians could look into the hearts of the gay community and understand the hardships that every one of us faces daily, perhaps they would treat them with more gentleness, patience, tolerance, and care. The most significant deficit we have in our society (and especially the evangelical church) is an empathy deficit. When you step into the shoes of your gay or lesbian loved one and walk, albeit momentarily, the life that they have lived, if you get as far as they have, just maybe you will see how strong they really are. Once you've stepped into the shoes of your gay loved one, aiming to understand their feelings and perspectives, you can now use that understanding to guide your actions.

THE CHOICE NO ONE CHOOSES

*"If you are a straight person and you genuinely believe that sexual orientation
is a choice, then you're not actually straight; you just haven't met
anyone persuasive enough yet."*
— Todd Glass

The sermons I heard in church growing up led me to believe that homosexuality was not just an abomination but also a lifestyle choice. I never understood that logic because I know I sure didn't choose to have this orientation. It also didn't sound like much of a choice among those gay individuals I observed from a distance. Yet the narrative that homosexuality is sinful is predicated on the belief that a person chooses to be gay. I don't know why anyone in their right mind, especially a Christ-follower, would choose something that would invite so much hatred, misunderstanding, and vitriol into their lives. Do some people really think that gays and lesbians see the oppression, the suicide rates, the discrimination and harassment, the inequality, the increased risk of mental health issues, or abandonment from your family and think to themselves, "Man, I gotta get me some of that"? This seems, to put it mildly, preposterous.

Is homosexuality really a choice that people make? The latest science has a lot to say regarding this question. Since the 19th century, many theories about the origin of homosexuality have been offered. Unfortunately, most are often untestable and contradictory.

The age-old question has been whether or not homosexual orientation is the result of nature or nurture. In other words, are people born gay, or do they become gay due to their upbringing or environmental factors? There was once the common belief that men became gay due to an absent father and/or an overbearing mother. There was also the ludicrous belief that the female homosexual had never fully recovered from her anger over not having a penis, and she wished to avenge her perceived castration by taking another female as her sexual object. Thankfully, our understanding of the origins of homosexual orientation has grown over the years.

Today's evidence shows that homosexuality is a natural, biological condition that someone is born with (nature) and that environmental factors (nurture) also play a role. So both nature and nurture are in play in the development of sexual orientation.

We now have strong evidence that there really is a significant genetic component to homosexuality. As sexual orientation has been studied in recent decades, scientists have looked at three main areas: genes, hormones, and birth order. But, of course, most of these studies focus only on male sexual orientation.

Let's first look at studies of identical twins. When one identical twin is a gay man, the other twin is also gay up to 70% of the time. Far higher than what would occur if genes played no role in this at all. In fact, these studies have found that genes play a more significant role in determining sexual orientation than they do of whether or not you're right or left-handed. [1]

In 1993, a study published in the journal Science showed that families with two homosexual brothers were very likely to have specific genetic markers on a region of the X chromosome known as Xq28. This led to media headlines about the possibility of the existence of a "gay gene" and discussions about the ethics of aborting a "gay" fetus. There have also been headlines about an "alcoholism gene" that makes people become alcoholics and a "warrior gene" that makes people unusually aggressive.[2]

It's also been discovered that the brain's structure might influence sexual preference. In 1991, a study showed that the hypothalamus, which controls the release of sex hormones from the pituitary gland, in gay men differs from the hypothalamus in straight men. The third interstitial nucleus of the anterior hypothalamus (INAH3) was found to be more than twice as large in heterosexual men as in homosexual men.[3]

Professor Michael Pepper, Director of the Institute for Cellular and Molecular Medicine at the University of Pretoria, South Africa, said that there is a strong association between a specific region of the X chromosome and male homosexuality. "This is not a choice," he said. "This happens very early on." It's not a mutation; it's very much like the genetic regions that determine whether you will have black or brown hair, whether you'll be tall or short, have dark or light skin, have broad or narrow hips… in other words, it is part of the normal range of normal human sexuality. And across all societies, the percentage of people who are gay remains about the same, at between 5-8%.[4]

"This is not a choice... it happens very early on."
-Dr. Michael Pepper

Scientists have also recently noticed a striking statistical phenomenon. Studies have also shown that having older brothers increases the odds of a boy being homosexual. And it's not because "Mom's always baby the youngest— making them gay." When a woman is pregnant with a boy, scientists are realizing that her female body often sees the male fetus as a foreign object. And her body begins to produce antibodies and antigens against it. Yet the more boys a woman has, the more adept her body becomes at feminizing the fetus. This may explain why the odds that a boy will be gay go up significantly with every successive male birth.

From an anthropological standpoint, this makes sense. It's believed by many experts that homosexuals were created for kin selection to benefit the advancement of mankind. When resources are constrained, or the environment is difficult, it benefits the family (more likelihood to pass on genes) if there is a gay sibling. Because the gay sibling doesn't need to use energy on procreating and bringing up their young, they can be charitable and use that energy to help their siblings. This may help explain why homosexuality is more likely when there are older siblings and more so in twins.

Let's take the Biblical character of Joseph, for example. He was the 11th son of Jacob. According to ancient Jewish commentaries known as the midrash, it was believed that Joseph and his half-sister Dinah were miraculously switched in the womb, meaning that they changed gender even before they were born. I thought that was interesting and worth noting. Perhaps this legend was invented to explain some feminine tendencies on behalf of Joseph. But there's an even more notable detail that's worth mentioning. The Bible says that Joseph's father, Jacob loved him more than his other children and had a special robe made for him. Today, we refer to this robe as the "coat of many colors." In Hebrew, the robe is called *ketonet passim*. Its meaning is considered unclear by many traditional Bible scholars. The only other use of the term is in 2 Samuel 13, where princess Tamar wears a *ketonet passim*. The author helpfully explains that this is "*how the virgin daughters of the king were clothed in earlier times.*" Traditional Bible scholars found it confusing that Joseph would wear an article of clothing that only female princesses would wear. Still, the meaning is plainly understandable to many of today's queer people of faith. Is it not surprising then why this may have been one of the factors that led Joseph's brothers to sell him into slavery? There is even a theory that the Egyptian officer Potiphar bought Joseph as a sex slave in order to satisfy his own desires, as was the custom and culture of that day. After all, we are told in Genesis 39:6 that Joseph was *"well built and handsome."* Perhaps this might explain why Joseph was able to refuse the sexual advances of Potiphar's wife, who tried to seduce him "day after day," and yet Joseph *"refused to go to bed with her or even be with her"* (Genesis 39:10). The Bible story goes on to tell how Joseph triumphed in the end, rising to become Egypt's second most powerful man and rescuing his family from starvation during a famine.

Was Joseph of a different orientation other than heterosexual? Of course, we can't say for sure. But these interesting nuances in the Biblical text lead us to scratch our heads and wonder. Regardless of his orientation, we are told that *"because the Lord was with Joseph* [God] *gave him success in whatever he did"* (Genesis 19:23).

Homosexuality in Nature

How many of us have been told all of our lives that homosexuality is unnatural? Is it really, though? Biology tells a different story. Homosexual behavior is common in over 1,500 different animal species. We've seen homosexual behavior and same-sex animal partnerships across the animal kingdom, including zebras, baboons, dolphins, sheep, dogs, elephants, horses, birds, gorillas, cats, rabbits, hedgehogs, and lions, to name a few. One of the animal species closest to us genetically, the bonobos, are 100% bisexual across the board. Same-sex penguin couples have been observed in nature for at least 100 years. At the Berlin Zoo, Skip and Ping are both male penguins, and they've been a couple for years. They recently "adopted" an abandoned egg at the

> Homosexual behavior has been observed in over 1,500 different animal species.

zoo and raised it together as their own offspring.[5] These are creatures that God created, and their behavior as a non-moral species is also the creation of God Himself. Animals have no sense of morality or what is right or wrong. And yet homosexual behavior comes very naturally to all of these species of God's creation. A behavior that is this ubiquitous across the animal kingdom is clearly of some tremendous ecological importance. So it's absolutely absurd to throw around words that homosexuality is "unnatural" when nature itself is clearly proving that assertion to be wrong.

Of course, the common objection is, "We're not animals. Human beings have free will." The problem is that you don't get to choose who you're attracted to.

Also, if homosexuality is so unnatural, why is the male g-spot (or p-spot) located where it is? It begs the question, why would God create the male body in the first place where the most erogenous pleasure center and the source of the most powerful, whole-body orgasms is located? Why is the male human body designed so that prostate-stimulated orgasms are reportedly 30 percent stronger than the average climax? Is our all benevolent God a trickster for creating something for pleasure and then banning its use? One could use this basic lesson in biology to build a case that perhaps it's not so unnatural at all.

As a pastor, I used to teach that being gay isn't a choice, but acting on those impulses certainly is. I no longer see the logic in my own past argument. We have indisputable evidence that a person can be born with homosexual tendencies. Why then would God allow a person to be born with these desires and then forbid them from ever being fulfilled? One gay friend told me recently that he grew to hate God by the time he was 16 years old. He couldn't understand why God would create a person with these gay desires only to have him destined to hell, knowing he could not change. This friend spent five years in conversion therapy with *Exodus International* (formerly the world's largest ex-gay ministry) before finally giving up and accepting his sexual orientation.

Whenever I have a conversation with people who believe that homosexuality is a choice, I always ask a simple yet straightforward question: "How old were you when you made the choice to be straight?" There's usually an awkward pause while they think about it, followed by a blank look on their face when they realize they don't have an adequate answer. They usually say, "Well, I've always been this way. I never had to make that decision." That's precisely the point. My response: "That's interesting. Do you think it may be the same way for gay people as well?"

Being gay isn't a choice, but choosing hate and misunderstanding certainly is.

> Being gay isn't a choice, but choosing hate and misunderstanding certainly is.

DRAWING LINES IN THE SAND

"The correct interpretation of scripture always comes down to how we love. The Bible's intent is not to be defended. The Bible was never intended to be this burden we carry. The Bible is a servant to Jesus. It's a helper of the Holy Spirit."
-- Derrick Flood, *Disarming Scripture*

The battle over human sexuality has become one of the most divisive issues facing Christianity in the West. Gallup found in 2001 that 40 percent of Americans felt homosexual relations were morally acceptable. It now stands at a record high of 70 percent of Americans now supporting same-sex marriage, including a majority of republicans.[1] That's an increase in 10 percentage points since 2015 when the U.S. Supreme Court ruled that all states must recognize same-sex marriages. I'm not asserting that popular opinion polls should shape our views on morality. But it does illustrate Americans' shifting view on this issue and the sharp divide of most conservative, evangelical leaders.

This has presented quite a dilemma for the modern evangelical church regarding how they're perceived by a watching world. Approximately 45,000 churches in the United States teach and believe that being LGBTQ is a sin. A 2007 study by the Barna Group, a Christian research firm, asked 16 to 29-year-olds to choose words and phrases to describe present-day Christianity. Among the many choices available to them were favorable terms like "offers hope" and "has good values" along with negative terms like "judgmental" and "hypocritical."

Out of all of it — good and bad — the most popular choice was "anti-homosexual." Not only did 91 percent of the non-Christians describe the church this way, but 80 percent of churchgoers did as well.[2] It's unfortunate how, in the 21st Century, the number one thing the church is now known for is being anti-gay. And we wonder why the Church isn't making any headway in influencing our nation's culture.

Not all, but many evangelicals hold onto their beliefs with such clenched fists that they fear and sometimes violently resist any questions and challenges to that belief system. That was me at one point. I feared that if I was wrong in my theological beliefs about something I was so certain — then what else could I have been wrong about? Would my faith come crashing down like a house of cards should the one card of "homosexuality = sin" be removed? That's what so many evangelicals fear — and therefore resist wanting to have a conversation about this topic.

But most Christians I know genuinely do want to be open-minded. When it comes to homosexuality and the Bible, the most prevalent posture that we see today is when good-hearted, well-intentioned Christians, who are doing their best to line their lives up with Scripture, are convinced that the Bible condemns homosexuality and same-sex relationships. Even though they want to support and remain in a close relationship with their gay loved ones, they know they must also honor their understanding of the Bible.

Colby Martin, author of the book, *Unclobber*, makes some good observations:

> When my friends Rebecca and Valerie, with their nine-month-old daughter Ella, are told that family members won't be coming to Thanksgiving because of their "sinful lifestyle," I think we're misusing the Bible.
>
> When LGBTQ youth are four times more likely to attempt suicide than their straight peers, and then eight times more likely to attempt suicide when they live in a home with a family that rejects them, I think we're misusing the Bible.
>
> When churches come out as fully welcoming and affirming and as a result are kicked out of their denominations, or watch as half their people leave, I think we're misusing the Bible.[3]

I'm writing this book because when you know better, you do better. As one gay friend aptly stated: "It's not the stab in the back that kills you. It's when you turn around and see who is holding the knife." The tragedy is that far too many LGBTQ people feel that it's the Church as well as well-intentioned loved ones, are the ones who are holding the knife.

> It's not the stab in the back that kills you, it's when you turn around and see who's holding the knife.

Archibald MacLeish said, "Religion is at its best when it makes us ask hard questions about ourselves. It is at its worst when it deludes us into thinking we have all the answers for everybody else."

Fear the Outsiders

We have a tendency to dehumanize people we disagree with. In our self-righteousness, we can quickly become the very things we dislike in others. It's true that some people have to pretend you're a bad person, so they don't feel guilty about the things they did to you.

It wasn't until 1973 that the American Psychiatric Association voted to remove homosexuality from its official list of mental disorders. Decades later, many people still treat those with same-sex attraction as if they are something to be feared, as though there is something fundamentally wrong with them. Dr. Mel White said, "So many people who are victims of the fundamentalist Christian caricature of gays become fearful and stay fearful until they meet one. Once they realize they have a gay cousin, or a lesbian aunt, or a transgender classmate — once they realize who we are up close and personal — that fear begins to go away."

The consequence of homophobia is that once you stereotype gay people, you then define them in negative ways. And once we do that, we're able to treat them negatively and brutally without any remorse. Fear does terrible things to society. When people are afraid, they have to find scapegoats, and then they want to get rid of those people that are the bad guys.

> The cheapest way of getting a tribe to rally together is to make an "other" – to find a common enemy.

The cheapest way of getting a tribe to rally together is to make an "other" — to find a common enemy. It's how we elect presidents in this country through polarizing politics. It's also why we malign entire demographics of people. Whether it be the black community during the Civil Rights era or the Jews during the period of anti-Semitism — our history has repeated this over and over again. Homosexuals are now, unfortunately, the new "other."

There's something about human nature to always want to look for an outsider… someone who is different. And when someone is different, we have a tremendous amount of fear and ignorance surrounding them. Gays have long been treated as the "whipping boy of sin" in American pulpits for far too long. By pointing a finger of accusation to the outsider — someone who "sins" differently than we do — we subconsciously feel better about ourselves, our own piety, and our own standing with God.

The voices of today's conservative Christian leaders have done much to propagate this attitude towards the gay community. Dr. James Dobson of *Focus on the Family* even went so far as to say that gays are comparable to Nazis and how they will destroy the Christian foundation of this country. He also said that Sandy Hook's school shooting was God's judgment on this nation because of gay marriage (Bennett-Smith, 2012).

Two days after the horrifying 9/11 terrorist attacks, the founder and chancellor of my alma mater, Liberty University, blamed gays in part for what he viewed as a sign of God's wrath on America, saying, "I point the finger in their face and say, you helped this happen."

Televangelist Pat Robertson responded by saying, "Well, I totally concur." However, both men later said they regretted the exchange.

The Church has become an enemy of the gay community because of outrageous statements from people like Pat Robertson touting that gay people wear rings so they can give you AIDS when you shake their hands (Sieczkowski, 2013).

Whenever one segment of the Church tries to build a bridge to the gay community (such as World Vision), the overwhelming reaction of the evangelical church has been disgust, hatred, and boycotting. Many Christians are afraid that allowing active homosexuals in their churches means allowing false doctrines and immorality or abandoning the faith altogether. This is simply not true.

Many people wrongly judge the gay community, believing that gay life revolves around endless sexual encounters, bars, nightclubs, dance parties, and drugs. People are taught by conservative Christian culture that homosexuality is nothing but promiscuity and orgies. No good-quality relationships but just one-night stands. This is often referred to by pastors and others as the "gay lifestyle." It's interesting to me that those who speak so knowledgeably about the "gay lifestyle" have never really sat down to have a conversation with gay men or lesbians. Their knowledge is gained by observation from elevated ecclesiastical towers constructed to separate them from the world Jesus called us to minister to. There is also a red light or nightclub area in every major city where straight people go and play. Yet, no one calls this a "heterosexual lifestyle." The party subculture exists equally in both gay and straight worlds alike. It's just easier to point the finger of accusation at the gays.

Gay people value the same things that heterosexuals do: love, friendships, happiness, companionship, intimacy, to make a difference where we can, and to treat people with respect.

Matthew J. Distefano raises an important question:

> Why does this topic cause such a stir within Christianity? One would think that Christians would be far more concerned with practicing compassion, kindness, humility, meekness, and patience (Col. 3:12), loving your enemies (Mark 11:25; Matt. 5:44; Luke 6:27), helping the poor (Matt. 19:21; Gal. 2:10), the orphans and widows (James 1:27), showing mercy and grace to the world (Matt. 9:13; Luke 6:36; John 8:1-11), and living in the Spirit, whose fruit includes love, peace, forbearance, kindness, goodness, faithfulness, gentleness, and self-control (Gal. 5:22-23). Is this not the overarching message of the Bible, particularly the New Testament? [4]

When I study the life of Christ, I find that Jesus seemed to want connection with those around Him, not separation. He touched human bodies deemed unclean as if they themselves were holy: dead little girls, lepers, menstruating women, even sex workers. The religious people of his day were disgusted by Jesus and his disciples and tried to shame Him for it. Jesus was loyal to the law, just not at the expense of the people.

As Nadia Bolz-Weber writes:

Jesus kept violating boundaries of decency to get to the people on the other side of that boundary, those who'd been wounded by it, those who were separated from the others: the motherless, the sex workers, the victims, and the victimizers. He cared about real holiness, the connection of things human and divine, the unity of sinners, the coming together of that which was formerly set apart.[5]

"Love the Sinner but Hate the Sin"

Every time I hear this statement, it makes me cringe on the inside. It seems like a nice platitude on behalf of conservative Christians. But when those within the gay community hear these words, all that they really hear is, "We secretly hate the essence of who you are." We've tried harder than you'll ever understand to separate and remove this orientation out of our lives. Yet, it's still there, and it's not going anywhere. So to hear a conservative Christian say that they love us but hate our "sin" — what we really hear is that we're not loved, and we're not accepted. It's like tying a pretty bow onto a dagger before driving it into our hearts.

> It's like tying a pretty bow onto a dagger before driving it into our hearts.

Step into the soul of a gay man or woman for a moment. For those of us who have grown up in religious homes, we too hated this "sin" so much that we also hated ourselves for it. Before we even had a conversation with you about this, we've sought help, fought it for years, denied it, and got on our knees and pleaded with God to take it away. When that never happened, the hate that we felt over the issue of our sexuality transformed into hatred for who we are as human beings. One's sexuality is near the very core of who they are — sexual orientation is rooted in our psychology and physiology. To hate being gay is to hate yourself. To despise one is to despise the other.

The Six Clobber Passages

Out of the 31,102 verses in the Old and New Testaments, you can count on two hands how many cover the topic of homosexuality. In reality, just 6 verses in the Bible speak even remotely of what we would refer to today as homosexual behavior. That's roughly 0.016% of the text. In contrast, the Bible contains more than 2,000 verses about money (and related issues of greed, wealth, loans, and property) and more than 100 verses specifically on one's obligation to care for widows. In other words, monitoring and proscribing human homosexual activity is not a particular concern of the Bible when compared to the overarching demand for justice, economic equality, and the fair treatment of foreigners and strangers. For certain Christian groups to make this the decisive Christian issue is simply a misreading of biblical values.

The LGBTQ community refers to these six Scriptures as "the clobber passages" because they feel as though they're continuously beaten up by the church with them. There are three in the Old Testament and three in the New.

The Old Testament:

- Genesis 19 — The story of Sodom and Gomorrah. God allegedly destroys these cities for their homosexual immorality.
- Leviticus 18:22 — "*Thou shalt not lie with mankind, as with womankind: it is abomination.*"
- Leviticus 20:13 — "*If a male lies with a male as with a woman, both of them have done what is detestable. They must be put to death; their blood is upon them.*"

The New Testament:

- Romans 1:26-27 — "*Because of this, God gave them over to shameful lusts. Even their women exchanged natural relations* for unnatural ones. In the same way the men also abandoned natural relationships with women and were inflamed with lust for one another."

- 1 Corinthians 6:9-10 — "Or do you not know that the unrighteous will not inherit the kingdom of God? Do not be deceived: neither the sexually immoral, nor idolaters, nor adulterers, nor men who practice homosexuality, nor thieves, nor the greedy, nor drunkards, nor revilers, nor swindlers will inherit the kingdom of God."

- 1 Timothy 1:9-10 — "understanding this, that the law is not laid down for the just but for the lawless and disobedient, for the ungodly and sinners, for the unholy and profane, for those who strike their fathers and mothers, for murderers, the sexually immoral, men who practice homosexuality, enslavers, liars, perjurers, and whatever else is contrary to sound doctrine…"

When I read those Scriptures as a young teen and later as a pastor, it seemed to me that God couldn't have been any more clear on this topic. This issue was not open to debate. Either I would believe what the Bible said to be true, or I would not. How can I argue with what's plainly written? I also thought that anyone who believed to the contrary — that homosexuality was permissible — was simply stretching and twisting Scripture to make it say what they wanted it to.

When my therapist asked me if I had ever investigated or listened to any other interpretations of these Scripture passages, my response was a quick and emphatic, "No." There was no use in my mind. The Bible made this issue a closed case. It wasn't until a whole year had passed after that conversation that I decided to maybe take a look and see how other people and churches that were "pro-gay" had understood the context, the

It felt like I had been set free from a prison of my own misinterpretation.

original language, and culture from which these passages were written. My mind was blown away by what I discovered. It felt like I had been set free from a prison of my own misinterpretation. How could I have pastored and struggled with this topic for so many years and never seen this? I say this as a Bible scholar who can read Hebrew and Greek and has two master's degrees and a doctorate degree from seminary. After discovering these insights, I knew this book had to be written because more people needed to see what was really going on beneath the surface of these Scriptures. There was an underlying reality not apparent from a cursory reading of our English translations today.

What I have found in my study of Scripture is that the Bible does not condemn homosexual orientation as we understand it today. On the contrary, every passage in the Bible that is traditionally used to condemn gays and lesbians are actually condemnations of sexual violence, rape, abuse, exploitation, and temple prostitution. And when I walk people through this who are deeply concerned about this issue — a light goes on in their hearts and minds.

When people believe that homosexuality is a sin in the eyes of God and that their view came directly from the Bible, what they really mean to say is that their view came from their interpretation of the Bible. Because the reality is every single one of us has a hermeneutic (a big word that encompasses the study of how we interpret the meaning of the Bible). In other words, every person has a lens through which they view Scripture. Technically speaking, we have a lens through which we view everything — so it's impossible to escape our own subjectivity when addressing so-called "objective truths." This is why not a single one of us has a purely biblical worldview. Instead, we have a worldview that is shaped by our subculture's interpretation of Christianity influenced by so many factors.

It's sad that such strong lines in the sand have been drawn over this issue. It's affected millions of people and separated LGBTQ individuals away from their families, friends, churches, and even their relationship with God. The reality is one of us is entirely wrong on this topic. If I am wrong, I have now led LGBTQ people to once again seek a relationship with a God who loves and accepts them just as they are. If the traditionalists are wrong, they have convinced gays that God doesn't want a relationship with them.

Gay men and women are taught by the church that they cannot accept who we are without putting our souls in jeopardy. But what if these lines in the sand don't have to be drawn? What if there really is a way that we can reconcile our faith in God with our understanding of the Bible? What if it's possible to have both a high view of Scripture, believing that God's Word is inspired…and be able to affirm and accept your gay loved one. It's not just possible; it's plausible when you examine the evidence. Jesus said, "*You shall know the truth, and the truth shall set you free*" (John 8:32). So let's examine these truths together.

GENESIS 19 – THE UNTOLD STORY OF SODOM

"Maybe Sodom and Gomorrah isn't really about homosexuality, but about rape. If the angels had been female, and the men of Sodom said they wanted to 'know' them against their will, would people claim that the story shows heterosexuality is a sin?"
— Alex Sanchez

A picket sign by the Westboro Baptist Church read: "In Genesis 19, God burned the cities of Sodom and Gomorrah because of homosexuality." I'm sure you've probably heard that by now. That's how we got the word "sodomy" after all — it's from this passage in Scripture. This passage in Genesis 19 is one that everyone (even if they don't read the Bible) is familiar with. Even Jay Leno said, "If God doesn't destroy Hollywood Boulevard, he owes Sodom and Gomorrah an apology." Most of us who grew up in church were taught about Sodom and Gomorrah in Sunday school. We were led to believe that God sent fire and brimstone from heaven to eradicate them for their homosexual practices in that day.

In the 18th chapter of Genesis, God says that He will destroy these two cities because He's heard that they're exceedingly wicked. And He sends two messengers, angels in the form of man. The following day, Abraham accompanies the two angels to Sodom and Gomorrah. He brings them to Lot's house, and Lot entertains them by giving them food, drink, and lodging. It was required among the Hebrew people back then that you were obligated to take a stranger in if they came to your door. There were no Holiday Inns for weary travelers to stay at in ancient times. If you were traveling, you had to rely on the hospitality and provisions of people who lived in the villages along the way towards your destination. So if someone knocked on your door — you were obligated to take them in. One of the most severe social breaches in the ancient day was not entertaining and caring for a stranger.

Sodom was an incredibly wealthy community, and they didn't want to share their wealth. They thought that if travelers passed through and were welcomed, they might want to come and steal their wealth. So they canceled the law of welcoming the travelers. Having violated the rule of Sodom, these wicked men came to the door of Lot and his angelic guests and threatened them. The Bible says in one translation, "Let these men come out so we can have sex with them." In another translation, it says, "Let these men come out so that we can know them."

What's really happening here is that these men wanted to gang rape these two strangers as an act of humiliation. In the ancient mind, the gang rape of men was a common way to humiliate, demean, and punish. Armies that would defeat other forces would commonly rape the defeated members of that opposing army.

Ancient people were prejudiced against outsiders. They would show that prejudice and demonstrate their superiority over them by enslaving people and sexually assaulting them.

The Sodom story is not about promiscuity or even perversity. According to the ancient rabbis, the story of Sodom was about cruelty and inhospitality. This narrative is not about homosexuality. This city was doomed for destruction before these angelic messengers arrived, and this incident happened.

> The Sodom story is not about promiscuity or even perversity. It's about cruelty and inhospitality. This narrative is not about homosexuality.

The Bible says that "*Lot went outside to meet them and shut the door behind him and said, 'No, my friends. Don't do this wicked thing. Look, I have two daughters who have never slept with a man. Let me bring them out to you, and you can do what you like with them. But don't do anything to these men, for they have come under the protection of my roof.*"

Once again, we see the strange patriarchal world in which the Bible was shaped. Lot offers his two daughters to be raped by the men of Sodom rather than giving up the two strangers he just met.

Rape, in the ancient world, was a tool of domination. Their interest wasn't sexual. It was to do harm. We're told that *every man in the entire city* surrounds the house and threatens these angels with gang rape. Ultimately, the angels blind the crowd and escape.

The real downfall of Sodom is not sodomy but inhospitality. But don't take my word for it. Let the Bible speak to answer this question of why Sodom was destroyed. The Prophet Ezekiel said, "*This was the guilt of your sister Sodom: she and her daughters had pride, excess of food, and prosperous ease, but did not aid the poor and needy. They were haughty, and did abominable things before me; therefore I removed them when I saw it*" (Ezekiel 16:49). Notice that there's no mention of sodomy or homosexuality.

Out of 20 biblical references to Sodom after Genesis 19, only 2 Peter 2:7 and Jude 7 even mention sexual sin but never specifically

No verse in the Bible says that God destroyed Sodom and Gomorrah because of homosexuality.

same-sex behavior. No verse in the Bible says that God destroyed Sodom and Gomorrah because of homosexuality.

But here is the question I would ask related to this story: is this narrative really about loving, committed homosexual relationships? Suppose these men had gang-raped Lot's daughters instead. Would we hold this story up to be about loving, committed, heterosexual relationships? Absolutely not. These men are threatening gang rape, not expressing romantic interest. This attack was not about homosexuality. It was their defiled way of demonstrating power over the outsiders and humiliating them so they would never return, all while violently gratifying their own sexual desires.

This account is reminiscent of Scott Howard, who was repeatedly raped by members of a prison gang called 211 Crew while serving time in the Colorado Department of Corrections. The 211 Crew was known for its vocal hatred of homosexuals. Yet they raped men in prison suspected of being gay. Rape was a means of demonstrating power and humiliation over others. What relationship does this kind of gang rape have to do with loving, committed relationships between two people of the same sex? None that I can see.[1]

There are a lot of towns all across America that are guilty of the sin of Sodom and Gomorrah. You can walk into these towns today, and the people won't show any signs of hospitality simply because you're black or gay or lesbian or just because you're an outsider. Unfortunately, many towns in rural America are just like that. We need to be reminded that that attitude is the very sin of Sodom and Gomorrah.

LEVITICUS 18 & 20 –
THE ABOMINATIONS

"Thou shalt not lie with mankind, as with womankind: it is abomination."
-- Leviticus 18:22

"If a male lies with a male as with a woman, both of them have done what is detestable. They must be put to death; their blood is upon them."
-- Leviticus 20:13

These passages seem crystal clear. It appears unmistakable that homosexuality is connected with being an abomination in the eyes of God. Yet context is key to understanding what any verse in Scripture means.

It's worth noting that the attempted gang-rape in Sodom is the only example of same-sex activity up to this point in Scripture. Could this have also been the backdrop behind these two passages in Leviticus? Given that this is the only occurrence of a *"man lying with a man,"* it's at least possible that Leviticus 18:22 and 20:13 were condemning homosexual rape rather than anything that resembles two people sharing their lives in a loving relationship.

What's even more probable though is that Moses is condemning the pagan use of temple prostitution or sex as worship and idolatry. Let's be honest. The Israelites were a little out of control after the Exodus from Egypt. Sex and idolatry were happening on the regular. While Moses was up on the mountain meeting with God, the Israelites got very nervous, made a golden calf and started having sex. As a rabbinical teacher, David Ben-Gad HaCohen notes:

> The terminology used in Exodus 32 implies that the Israelites were involved in group sexual promiscuity…the dancing and sex that happens, seems to be a ritual where the divine couple, El (represented by the calf/bull) and Asherah (El's wife), are being worshipped together. [1]

You have to understand that the context to why these Levitical laws were written was that temple sex, orgies, and prostitution were the background that the Israelites were coming from. Men having sex with men and women with women was an element of the Egyptian occult rituals. If that surprises you, it also surprised Herodotus, the ancient historian who writes:

> And these same priests claim — though it sounds incredible to me — that the god himself visits the temple and sleeps on the bed, just as the Egyptians claim that the same thing happens in Egyptian Thebes for there, too, the woman lies in the temple of Theban Zeus, and both women are said to engage in intercourse with no human men at all.

This is why Moses had to get absolutely specific about not aligning their behavior with the pagan and idolatrous usages of sex. In Deuteronomy 23:17-18, he says, *"None of the daughters of Israel shall be a temple prostitute; none of the sons of Israel shall be a temple prostitute. You shall not bring the fee of a prostitute or the wages of a male prostitute into the house of the Lord your God in payment for any vow, for both of these are abhorrent to the Lord your God."* This is likely the only model known for sex between two men up to this point. So in essence, Moses is prohibiting men from visiting pagan male temple prostitutes and practicing idolatry.

It's also worth noting that this idea of a "man lying with man" scenario in these Leviticus passages could also be directed to married men committing adultery with another male. So it's not describing what we would understand to be a sexual orientation.

The 18th chapter of Leviticus begins a set of prohibitions meant to separate the people of Israel from the pagan cultures that surround them. Leviticus 18:2-3 says, "*Speak to the Israelites and say to them…You must not do as they do in Egypt…*" These prohibitions are meant to call them away from looking and acting like the pagan idolatrous culture they had been surrounded with while in captivity. Verse 21 says, "*Do not give any of your children to be sacrificed to Molek.*" Once again, we see how all of these prohibitions were in response to the Egyptians' idolatry and pagan worship culture.

There was another issue pertaining to the Israelites that may have surrounded this issue — the need for procreation. This is about a nation that was trying to grow. At the time, the ancient Hebrew people understood that male seed was all of life contained right there. Women had nothing to contribute to the birth process other than to be an incubator for the male seed. So this particular verse may have been directed towards the intention of saving male seed to procreate so that the nation of Israel could grow and expand. There is no ability to reproduce when you are engaged in homosexual behavior. So some speculate that it could have been a violation of the cultural needs at that time.

Ish vs. Zachar

The following observation is perhaps the most legitimate interpretation of these verses. When you examine how Leviticus 20:13 is worded in its original Hebrew language, it presents another interesting caveat of what is and is not there. The text prohibits a sexual relationship between a "man" (*ish* in Hebrew) and a male (*zachar* in Hebrew), not between an "*ish*" and another "*ish*."

That may sound like splitting hairs, but every word counts where the Torah is concerned. So why is this particular word for "male" used in this verse? It's possible that this isn't a prohibition against male sexuality but instead of pederasty or child pedophilia? As we will repeatedly see in this book, the ancient world was known for a popular and common social practice that we would all find abhorrent today. It was customary for men to mingle with young boys — in a context where mentoring, socializing, partying, and sexual activities would occur between the two groups. We know from archaeology that the Babylonians practiced keeping a temple sex "servant," an oftentimes prepubescent boy (because they were more feminine) would be enslaved to perform certain duties not just to the high priest/priestess, but also for engaging in fertility fornication rituals. There is heavy historical and archaeological evidence to support the claim that these were the pederasty practices being condemned here in Leviticus.

This word *zachar* is used 82 times in the Pentateuch alone and can be translated either as a noun or an adjective. In 77 out of those 82 verses, it describes male children who specifically have no rights. You can check any lexicon, and you'll find the first most common definition of *zachar* is a young boy that is still a minor or one who does not have rights. *Zachar* is also used to refer to infants for circumcision in most passages. Archaeology also tells us it was a common pagan practice to molest minors for the pagan god Molek and have massive orgy rituals with young boys. It's worth noting also that Leviticus 18:22 also uses the word *zachar* rather than *ish*. If these verses were meant to refer to adult homosexual behavior, then the wording in both Leviticus 18 and 20 would require that *ish>ish* be used, not *ish>zachar*. It's, therefore, safe to assume that Leviticus is referring to a pedarastic relationship which is an evil that everyone, regardless of sexual orientation, can agree upon.

What exactly is an "abomination?"

"God calls homosexuality an abomination." The church has heard this phrase so much that it reminds me of what Inigo Montoya said in the movie *The Princess Bride*: "You keep using that word. I do not think it means what you think it means." It's also reminiscent of what Gebel said working for the Nazi regime in Germany, "If you tell a lie enough times, the whole world will believe it."

When the term "abomination" is used in the Hebrew Bible, it always addresses a ritual wrong. It's not used to refer to something that is innately immoral. The idea of "abomination" (*toevah* in Hebrew) were acts that were may have been linked to idolatry. Eating pork is not innately immoral... but it was an abomination. It was a violation of a ritual requirement. There were even certain abominations that Scripture says were okay for the surrounding people groups to do — just not the Israelites.

These Biblical laws within Leviticus comprise what is known as the "holiness code." They were laws that were supposed to help the Israelites find distinctiveness in their new lives from the surrounding culture.

Some Biblical scholars argue that the Book of Leviticus was not originally meant to apply to the general public: its laws were meant only for the Levites (one tribe of Israel) who were meant to be the priests for the Temple. Chapter 21 explicitly hands down rules that apply specifically to priests, such as bans on ritual scarring and tattoos. The priests and their families were expected to adhere to higher norms. For example, chapter 21 states, "*They must not marry women defiled by prostitution or divorced from their husbands.*" Historians tell us that the entire Book of Leviticus and its rules on food, clothing, and behavior were initially meant exclusively for the priests. That is, until the period of Babylonian captivity. Eventually, some from the Levite class in Babylon found a way to encourage the Jewish people living in exile to take on these laws to keep them together as a community. Keeping these customs would have given the Jewish people a unique identity that separated them from the non-Jews living in Babylon. The more you study the historical context of how the Bible was formed, the more you see how these prohibitions (and who they did and did not apply to) evolved over hundreds of years.

There are far more verses forbidding what most Christians now eat at a church potluck than there are verses that appear to condemn homosexuality.

There are tons of things described by the Law of Moses as an abomination that we would not consider unclean or abnormal today. For example, eating pork or seafood was an abomination in ancient times. Still, none of us assume that's a violation of God's will for us now. There are far more verses in the Bible forbidding what most Christians eat today at a church potluck than there are verses that appear to condemn homosexuality.

For some strange reason, the kind of Christians who want to condemn gays and lesbians never talk about the other abominations in the Bible. Maybe it's because many of these lesser discussed abominations directly affect them as they commit these acts, perhaps daily. For example, in just a few verses above and below this one, Moses teaches that…

- It is an abomination to eat shrimp, lobster, scallops, etc. (Leviticus 11:10)
- You shouldn't plant two seeds in the same hole or commingle your crops (Leviticus 19:19).
- Having sex with your wife while she's still on her menstrual period was an abomination (Leviticus 18:19).

- It is an abomination to eat a rabbit (Leviticus 11:6).
- Getting a tattoo (Leviticus 19:28).
- Charging interest on loans...I hope no one reading this works for a bank (Deuteronomy 23:19).
- Eating any animal that walks on all four legs is an abomination (Leviticus 11:42). No more hamburgers.
- There's another rule that you shouldn't wear garments that have mixed fabrics together, such as weaving linen and wool together (Lev. 19:19; Deut. 22:11). If you're wearing any type of modern clothing right now while reading this, you're violating this command.
- You've committed an abomination if you've eaten bacon, ham, sausage, ribs, or a pork sandwich (Isaiah 66:17).
- We're commanded to stone women to death if they are found to have lost their virginity prior to their wedding night (Deut. 22:13-21).
- Certain types of haircuts such as rounding the corners of your heads are forbidden (Leviticus 19:27).

All Christians today have no problem disregarding these prohibitions. Yet, some will cling to the ones presumably against homosexuality as if their very lives depended on it. We fall into great error when we fail to read the Bible within the context of its authors and of its original culture. Fundamentalist Christians today are guilty of doing what they've accused others of doing: *selective reading of the Scriptures*. What happens is that when people already have a belief about something, they look back into the Bible and find reasons or justifications for that belief.

Pastors like me used to say, "You can't just treat the Bible like a cafeteria line and pick and choose what verses you want to believe are relevant." But the reality is, every single one of us does — regardless of whether you're conservative or progressive in your theological beliefs. What we have done is essentially picked two verses out of

Leviticus and said, "These are the ones that are the most important. We're just gonna ignore all the rest of these prohibitions that aren't followed today." That's hypocritical. Either you include all of the prohibitions into your practice, or you don't.

Just Keep the Moral Laws?

I used to argue that we may cut the ceremonial and cultural laws out of the Bible, but we must keep the moral ones. In other words, we as Christians can do away with anything "Jewish," but we are to retain the moral precepts taught in the Bible. However, as Dr. Benjamin L. Corey reminds us, things aren't so cut and dried:

> This argument presupposes that the Law is divided into categories — mainly dietary, morality, and ceremony. Unfortunately, the Law is not sorted into categories. The Law itself does not identify different categories, neither is it written in a way where the laws are sorted into clean and separate categories. For example, there's not a book of food laws followed by a book of moral laws—it's simply not written this way. Can we sort them into categories? Sure, but only for pedagogical purposes, nothing more.[2]

The Apostle Paul takes this one step further. He tells the church that if they insist on following one law (in his example, male circumcision), they have to follow them all (Gal. 5:3). So if we want to anachronistically impose the Law when it comes to marriage rites, are we also willing to impose all of these other 613 Biblical laws onto ourselves and others as well? Paul also said that he himself was not under the Law (1 Cor. 9:20) and that it had been canceled when it was nailed to the cross (Col. 2:14).

Robert Gagnon, associate professor of New Testament at Pittsburgh Theological Seminary who has spent much of his career studying and writing in condemnation of homosexuality readily admits:

I do not doubt that the circles out of which Leviticus 18:22 was produced had in view homosexual cult prostitution, at least partly. Homosexual cult prostitution appears to have been the primary form in which homosexual intercourse was practiced in Israel.

Regardless of the reasons why Leviticus condemns same-sex relations, we need to be reminded that the entire Old Testament law code has never applied to Christians in light of Christ's death. With Jesus, we don't have these antiquated laws anymore (thank God). Hebrews 8:13 says that Jesus made these Old Testament laws *"obsolete and outdated and will soon disappear."* Romans 10:4 says that *"Christ is the end of the law."* Christians have never regarded all of the Old Testament laws as being universally applicable today. So the Old Testament doesn't settle the issue of homosexuality for Christians.

ROMANS 1 –
ROME GONE WILD!

"For this reason God gave them up to dishonorable passions. For their women exchanged natural relations for those that are contrary to nature; and the men likewise gave up natural relations with women and were consumed with passion for one another, men committing shameless acts with men and receiving in themselves the due penalty for their error."
- Romans 1:26-27

Out of the six passages that appear to mention homosexuality, this was the one that was the most challenging for me to understand from an affirming standpoint. I could fully explain and understand the Old Testament passages and the other two New Testament passages easily. Still, this one in Romans was the most challenging one for me to look at with a fresh perspective. In my opinion, this Scripture is by far the most significant passage in the homosexuality debate. One gay man named Josh said, "I still can't get past Romans. The Old Testament passages are no problem, and the two verses in Corinthians and Timothy seem easy to explain. But I can't yet get past the passage in Romans that appears to condemn me as a gay man." [1]

Paul's words in Romans chapter one have long haunted gay people. This text contains the longest reference to same-sex behavior in the Bible. Many people point to the Book of Romans as the text that brought them to faith in Christ. But for countless LGBTQ people, Romans is the book that has driven many of them away from their faith and sent them down a path of despair.

When we examine this passage, we need to understand why Paul wrote what he did. What was the underlying principle he was proscribing based on that day's historical and cultural context — particularly in Rome? Once that question is answered, then we can figure out how to apply his words faithfully today.

Idolatry

Verse 26 begins with *"Because of this..."* What is the "because" there for? What is it that's causing these men and women to exchange natural relations? Paul says they exchanged the truth of God for a lie. They worshipped created things instead of the Creator God. Paul condemns Roman idolatry and temple prostitution, where men and women would offer themselves as sexual sacrifices to appease the gods and goddesses. Romans 1 is all about the descent of pagan culture and its idolatrous practices. Sometimes it was homosexual sex, and sometimes it was heterosexual sex — but all of it was idolatrous sex. None of that is what LGBTQ people practice today.

This passage is describing people who had turned away from God towards idolatry.

This passage is describing people who had turned from God, refusing to give God honor or thanks and had worshipped idols instead. God responded by giving them over to sexual immorality, resulting in their abandoning *"natural"* (heterosexual?) sex in exchange for committing *"shameless acts"* with each other. On the surface, it makes it sound like God gave people over to homosexuality as a result of their turning away from Him. But, did that mean that these straight people became gay when they turned from God?

I can identify with how Justin Lee relates himself to this passage:

> I hadn't turned away from God. I was sure I hadn't turned from God. I knew I wasn't perfect, but I certainly had never turned away the way this passage seemed to suggest. How could it say that my being gay was a punishment for turning from God? And if other Christians read this, no wonder they thought I was some kind of apostate.[2]

It seems at face value, regardless of the interpretation of the Old Testament passages, that the enduring truth of the ages is that God is against same-sex relations. But is that really what's going on here? Once again, we hear echoes of the Old Testament view of what was clean and unclean, natural and unnatural, acceptable or detestable. When Paul takes up this issue regarding same-sex relations, he seems to have in mind at least two of the ideas we discussed in the previous chapter: ritual sexual encounters tied to pagan worship/idolatry and the idea of what was clean/unclean or natural/unnatural. We know this because these verses are set in the context of Paul's condemnation of idolatry (see vs. 25... the verse immediately preceding this text in question). Paul connects this dishonorable sex as a direct result of idol worship, not once, but twice. It's more likely that Paul is describing the ritual prostitution practiced in pagan temples once again. The behavior being described here is about performing unnatural acts to appease and gain the favor of these false gods. *"They"* was a reference to people who had turned from God and become idol worshippers. Paul used them and their sexual cultic rites as an illustration to make a point to his audience.

In vs. 21, Paul says, *"although they knew God, they neither glorified him as God nor gave thanks to him."* In their rebellious ways, they created images of worship. They took out a knife and carved a tree branch into a god, and they bowed down and worshipped an image they had created. They took this into the temple and committed a sexual sacrifice to their god. Adultery, orgies, and all sorts of shameful and unnatural things were taking place in these temples. As we've seen over and over again, cult prostitution was one of the primary ways ancient pagans worshipped their gods (see Deut. 23:17-18, 1 Kings 14:24, 15:12, 22:47, 2 Kings 23:7).

This does not represent gay Christians today. If this passage were about gay people, it would mean that people are gay because they reject a relationship with God. That is certainly not true for myself or any of the gay Christian friends that I know. So many Christians love Jesus and still find themselves attracted to the same sex naturally. So the reality of the world around us makes that interpretation fall flat.

> If this passage were about gay people, it would mean that people are gay because they reject a relationship with God.

Dishonorable Passions

Romans 1:26 says that *"God gave them over to dishonorable passions."* The NIV uses the phrase *"shameful lusts."* Paul's words here are clearly negative. But when you understand this context, you can see why he names this behavior as lustful. He makes no mention of love, commitment, or faithfulness. His description of same-sex behavior is solely based on a burst of excess and lust.

In Greek, the word used here for *"passions"* or *"lust"* is *atimia*. If something was *atimia*, it wasn't so much about being morally reprehensible. It was used in reference to what was culturally shameful. It was about bringing dishonor to a person or a family. In a court of law, if something was deemed *atimia*, it was because it had no worth or value. To commit *atimia* meant that you were engaging in behavior that had no value and would bring shame and dishonor to you. It was a violation of a cultural custom of that day. And it's also very similar to the idea of the Hebrew word *toevah*, which is translated as "abomination." We can't assume that *atimia* means inherently wrong or evil because of how Paul uses it in other verses. For instance, in 1 Corinthians 11:14, Paul told the church, *"Does not even nature teach you that if a man wears long hair it is a disgrace* [atimia] *for him?"* Having long hair was not morally wrong, vile, or evil. In the Jewish culture, it was just seen as dishonorable, an act that violated the cultural custom of the day.[3] Yet, in the Old Testament, men were praised and admired for having long hair.[4] What was considered *"natural"* in the culture of the Old Testament was now considered *"unnatural"* within the New. Nearly all Christians today interpret Paul's words, not as a command for how men today need to cut their hair — but as a cultural convention during that time.

Paul demonstrated how these Gentiles were engaged in acts that weren't in line with Jewish cultural customs. They were *atimia* — disgraceful and shameful. Similarly, in our country — allowing the American Flag to touch the ground or be trampled on is an example of what would be to us, *atimia*. It is an act perceived as dishonorable and shameful. No one would ever suggest such an act is morally evil or that it offends the nature of God, but in our culture, it's a disgraceful act.

Shameless Acts

Paul goes on to say in verse 27, "*the men…were consumed with passion for one another, men committing shameless acts with men.*" The Greek word for "shameless" is *aschemosune*, and it describes a type of behavior that is improper and indecent. These were men who, overtaken by their passions, were engaging in same-sex acts possibly performed in public spaces and/or in conjunction with pagan temple idol worship. Both of those would have clearly been seen as inappropriate or indecent.

I would never argue that Paul didn't have harsh words to say about sexual behavior between two individuals of the same sex (or opposite sex, for that matter). What I am arguing for is a more nuanced approach that sees Paul condemning the forms of same-sex acts that were most prevalent in his day. We're not comparing apples to apples when we take his prohibitions and use them as a blanket condemnation of the LGBTQ community today. The New Testament speaks negatively about tax collectors. Still, we don't view that as a condemnation for anyone working for the IRS today. We understand that it refers to the common corrupt practices of the tax collectors of Jesus' day.

In his book *God and the Gay Christian*, Matthew Vines makes a compelling argument that these "shameless acts" were done as a result of men being "consumed with passion." They were not acting out of a place of love and mutuality but out of a desire for lustful excess.

Several decades ago, historian John Boswell noted that Paul was condemning same-sex behavior that was practiced by heterosexual people. According to Boswell's research, Paul denounced same-sex behavior because it was unnatural to the individuals engaging in it. Most of the men engaging in these acts had a wife at home (or more than one wife). This view is compelling because Paul says that they "exchange" or "abandon" the opposite sex for same-sex relations. Perhaps it's reasonable to think that Paul was condemning, as Boswell argued, "homosexual acts committed by apparently heterosexual persons." [5] The concepts of a person's homosexual orientation and egalitarian same-sex relationships — simply didn't exist in Paul's world. In general, people were thought to be capable of both opposite-sex and same-sex attraction. In the first century, same-sex relations were not thought to be the expression of a sexual orientation. They were widely understood to be the product of excessive sexual desire in general. The most common forms of same-sex behavior in the Greco-Roman world were pederasty, prostitution, and sex between masters and slaves — the majority of men indulging in these practices were also engaged in heterosexual behavior. This is why Plato argued for the banning of same-sex relations in Ancient Greece because it would positively impact "the loving bond between husbands and their wives," indicating that men who engaged in same-sex behavior were most commonly married to women.

> The most common forms of same-sex behavior in the Greco-Roman world were pederasty, prostitution, and sex between masters and slaves.

As New Testament professor James Brownson has written: "What is degrading and shameless about the behavior described in Romans 1:24-27 is that it is driven by excessive, self-seeking lust, that it knows no boundaries or restraints, and that it violates established gender roles of that time and culture, understood in terms of rationality and honor." None of these traits extend to the loving, committed relationships of gay Christians today.

In Paul's day, same-sex relations were a potent symbol of sexual excess. The specific example Paul drew from his culture doesn't have the same resonance when we compare it to same sex Christian couples now. From the church's early centuries through the nineteenth century, commentators consistently identified the moral problem in Romans 1:26-27 as *"unbridled passions,"* not the expression of same-sex orientation.[6] What Paul is describing is fundamentally different from what we are discussing. Gay Christians today don't pursue same-sex relationships because they're bored with their wives and seek a new outlet for their insatiable lusts. They pursue same-sex relationships for the same reasons straight Christians pursue opposite-sex relationships. They desire intimacy, companionship, and long-term commitment.

Natural vs. Unnatural

The Greek phrase for *"contrary to nature"* or *"unnatural"* is *para phusis*, meaning "against nature." The modern traditional interpretation of this passage is that the idolatrous Gentiles are turning away from God in idolatry and abandoning natural sexual relations for those that went against nature. In this perspective, God's design (according to the creation account of God creating one man and one woman) is for men to have sex with women. This is the natural way. This viewpoint would also say that any other sexual expression is unnatural.

There is much truth to that assertion. In the ancient world, if a man took the active role in sex, his behavior was deemed "natural." But if he took the passive role, he was criticized for engaging in "unnatural" sex. The opposite was also true for women. They were expected to be sexually passive as that was "natural," while sexual dominance for them was "unnatural." According to Plato, same-sex behavior was shameful to some in first-century culture because it involved "weakness and effeminacy" for one of the participants engaged in same-sex activity. In a patriarchal society that had great detest for anything that appeared to be related to women, the passive or receptive partner was seen as being less than a man. First-century

Jewish writer Josephus said that women were "inferior in every respect," so to take on a receptive role in sex was "unnatural" as the man would also become inferior to another man. In Plato's words, it was contrary to nature to allow themselves "to be covered and mounted like cattle" [7] by another man. It was this cultural view of women being inferior to men that became the main objection to same-sex behavior as it required, in the words of Philo, "those who [are] by nature men to submit to play the part of women." [8] According to Philo, femininity was a "disease." In ancient Jewish writings, women were also warned not to "imitate in any way the sexual role of men." [9] A third-century Greek text taught that "neither should the female be masculinized contrary to nature nor too should the male be softened in an improper manner." [10] These ancient texts show us how the words "natural" and "unnatural" were understood in the writings of that day. They weren't synonyms for straight and gay. As Matthew Vines says, "They were boundary markers between what did and didn't conform to customary gender roles in a patriarchal context. In fact, some interpreters argue that Romans 1:26 doesn't even refer to female same-sex relations, but to heterosexual sex that was considered "unnatural" because a woman was in the dominant position." It was these patriarchal views of women that shaped the ancient categories of "natural" and "unnatural" sex used in Romans 1.

In its simplest explanation, the best way to understand *para phusis*, the Greek word for "unnatural" or "contrary to nature" (and the converse, *kata phusis*, "natural" or "according to nature), is to understand what these words meant at that time. In the context of sexual relations, it dealt not so much with what was "moral" but rather with what was procreative and what was non-procreative. Just because something was *para phusis* didn't always mean it was evil or immoral. Paul used the word "nature" to refer to what we understand as "custom." The roots of these phrases *kata/para phusis* go back to

Plato, are picked up 300 years later by Philo (Jewish philosopher), and then Paul.

To illustrate this point, Augustine wrote that when a man has sex with a prostitute, while it was not praiseworthy, at least it was "according to nature." It was not moral, but at least it was natural. Then Augustine said, "But if one has relations even with one's wife in a part of the body which was not made for begetting children [i.e. anal or oral sex], such relations are against nature and indecent." This was the cultural thinking of that time.

This understanding is significant because many will point to Romans 1 as the Bible's primary condemnation of lesbianism. But that's not how the church would have understood Paul's words either.

Colby Martin writes:

> "Women exchanging natural relations (i.e., procreative sexual acts) for those that are contrary to nature (i.e., non-procreative sexual acts) most certainly was intended to mean anal heterosexual intercourse with men, not sexual relations between two women. Up through the fourth century, church fathers who commended on Romans 1:26 understood Paul in this way. Not referring to lesbianism, but referring to men and women having sex in unnatural ways (that is, non-procreative sexual intercourse)... So, what we can say is that then having sex with men (also men having anal/oral sex with women) was seen as contrary to nature in the ancient Jewish perspective because it was non-procreative." [11]

In Romans 11, Paul talks about how the olive tree is a metaphor for Israel, and the branches are the Gentiles that are being grafted into God's redemption plan. The word that Paul used to describe how God grafted us in is *para phusis*. Just because a particular action is called "unnatural" or "contrary to nature" doesn't necessarily make it inherently evil or immoral. If it did, Paul would be saying that God acted in evil and wicked ways.

When Paul uses the phrase "contrary to nature" or the words "natural" and "unnatural" in the New Testament, he's simply meaning what is customary and what is uncustomary. In ancient societies, male passivity or female dominance in sex was seen as "unnatural" because it violated patriarchal norms. However, those norms were also culturally limited. It wasn't customary for men to have sex with men in the Jewish context. But it was widespread in the Greek world. And Paul saw that as evidence of worshipping the wrong God... of idolatry.

Paul's only reference for this, of course, is that of exploitive same-sex relationships among the pagan Romans and Greeks. Those are the very people he's talking about in this passage. Paul had never contemplated the kind of monogamous, long-term relationships that are very much normal among homosexual people today.

The Bible really doesn't deal with the modern concept of homosexuality because it has so little reference for it. Therefore the few references that have been lifted out of the Bible to be used in religious teachings to condemn homosexuals really are inappropriate.

> The Bible doesn't deal with the modern concept of homosexuality because it has so little reference for it.

Like most ancient cities that day, the ancient Romans were unhinged when it came to their sexual lifestyles. As we've seen, in the ancient Greco-Roman world, most of the depictions we have of same-sex behavior was what mainly occurred between grown men and adolescent boys, between masters and their slaves, or in prostitution. Most of the men engaged in those practices were married to women. So same-sex behavior was viewed in the early church as wild and unrestrained lust. This was so common in ancient times that the Romans often wore a winged erect penis around their necks to represent one of their gods in the same way that Christians today wear a cross around theirs. Same-sex behavior was seen as a vice of excess like gluttony or drunkenness.

In summary, Romans 1 refers to lustful same-sex behavior — not to loving, monogamous relationships. From the church's early centuries through the nineteenth century, commentators consistently identified the moral problem in Romans 1:26-27 as "unbridled passions," not the expression of same-sex orientation. As the fifth-century Christian bishop Julian of Eclanum explained it, Paul was contrasting those who make a "right use" of sexual desire with those "abandoned persons [who] indulge" in the "excess of it." For Julian, the moral of the Romans 1 passage was this: "He who observes moderation in natural [desire] uses a good thing well; but he who does not observe moderation abuses a good thing." [12]

> The New Testament mentions of same-sex behavior are always connected with sex being offered to gods and goddesses as an act of pagan worship prevalent in the ancient world.

The New Testament mentions of same-sex behavior are always connected with sex being offered to gods and goddesses as an act of pagan worship prevalent in the ancient world. Male and female prostitutes would serve the people coming to these pagan temples through cultic rituals involving orgies and idol worship. The non-procreative sex acts (men with men, or anal/oral sex with women) practiced by these idol-worshipping pagans were viewed as culturally offensive to the Jewish people who acted in shameless and indecent ways. It's about idolatry and sexual exploitation. Romans 1 literally tells us this. It says that they *"exchanged the glory of the immortal God for images resembling mortal man and birds and animals and creeping things...they exchanged the truth about God for a lie and worshiped and served the creature rather than the Creator"* (Romans 1:23-26). As with anything, context is crucial. As Jarrod Saul McKenna reminds us, "A text without a context is a con."

Does this description in Romans 1 have anything to do with your friend or family member who might identify as gay and a follower of Jesus Christ? What do a few verses about people accused of turning their backs on God, worshipping idols, and giving into their excessive lusts have to say about them? The Romans passage, on the surface, may appear to be the most difficult one to overcome. But, once you fully understand the historical and cultural context, you realize it has nothing to do with today's gay Christians.

1 CORINTHIANS 9 & 1 TIMOTHY 1 – GAYS AND THE KINGDOM OF GOD

"Do you not know that wrongdoers will not inherit the kingdom of God? Do not be deceived! Fornicators, idolaters, adulterers, male prostitutes [malakoi], sodomites [arsenokoitai], thieves, the greedy, drunkards, revilers, robbers — none of these will inherit the kingdom of God."
— 1 Corinthians 9:9-10

"We also know that the law is made not for the righteous but for lawbreakers and rebels, the ungodly and sinful, the unholy and irreligious, for those who kill their fathers or mothers, for murderers, 10 for the sexually immoral, for those practicing homosexuality, for slave traders and liars and perjurers—and for whatever else is contrary to the sound doctrine that conforms to the gospel concerning the glory of the blessed God, which he entrusted to me."
-- 1 Timothy 1:9-11

Will gay people inherit the kingdom of God? That was a questionable fear I've always had. I wanted nothing more than to be included in God's plan for the world and be assured that I went to heaven when I died... so this fear led me to "pray the sinner's prayer" for salvation more times than I could count as a child. In 1 Corinthians, Paul warns that people who persist in sin will not inherit the kingdom of God. In his list of wrongdoings, he includes two Greek words that connect to some forms of same-sex behavior. But what is he talking about exactly? This passage has been referred to as the most dangerously mistranslated verse in the Bible. In his book, *Forging a Sacred Weapon: How the Bible Became Anti-Gay*, Ed Oxford writes how the English Bibles were changed to exclude an entire group of people. So in this chapter, we'll examine both of those words: *malakoi* and *arsenokoitai*.

Malakoi

In 1 Corinthians 6:9, the word the NKJV translates as "homosexuals" is translated as *"male prostitutes"* in the NRSV. It comes from the Greek word *malakoi* but hardly means what we mean when we say "homosexual." In Matthew 11:8 and Luke 7:25, Jesus describes some clothing as *malakoi*. It was a word that could also mean "soft" or "effeminate." In the Bible it is commonly used to describe fancy clothing. Plato and Josephus used the word to describe those men who were not fit for battle. When Aristotle used the word, he referred to those who over-indulged in pleasure. Many other sources outside the Bible used *malakoi* to refer to cult prostitutes.

The New American Bible offers the following definition:

> [Malakoi] may refer to catamites, i.e., boys or young men who were kept for purposes of prostitution, a practice not uncommon in the Greco-Roman world. In Greek mythology, this was the function of Ganymede, the "cupbearer of the gods," whose Latin name was Catamitus. The term translated "sodomites" refers to adult males

who indulged in homosexual practices with such boys. See similar condemnations of such practices in Romans 1:26-27; 1 Timothy 1:10. [3]

The place of slavery in the sexual landscape of classical antiquity could hardly be overestimated. The slave trade was in fact driven by the demand for commodified sexual availability. There was a widespread tradition at the time for Roman citizens to have a *pias* or catamite on the side (other than their spouse). This was known that day as an eromenos-erastes relationship. They could be condemned explicitly because of their power difference and enslavement.

It's important to note that in Matthew 8:5-13, Jesus heals a Roman centurion's *pias* or slave boy. It's suspected that this word was used here because this boy was a sex slave, and this term was commonly used to refer to them. Jesus heals the centurion's *pias* and commends the centurion for his faith.

As we've already seen, the concept of "homosexuality" was not present in Paul's day, at least not in the modern way we understand it. So when Paul speaks of these "unnatural" acts between same-sex partners, it seems plausible that he's speaking to something else entirely that was relevant to the culture of the first century.

Pastor John Shore explains:

> During the time in which the New Testament was written, the Roman conquerors of the region frequently and openly engaged in homosexual acts between themselves and boys. Such acts were also common between Roman men and their slaves. These acts of non-consensual sex were considered normal and socially acceptable. They were, however, morally repulsive to Paul, as today they would be to everyone, gay and straight.[2]

Sarah Ruden also echoes this point in her book, *Paul Among the People*, where she makes the strong case that whenever Paul discusses "homosexuality," it is in the context of pederasty running rampant in the Greco-Roman world.

> Sexual relationships in the ancient world — not just between men and men but between men and women — tended to be hierarchical: meaning that the penetrated was subservient to the penetrator. In that regard, being on the receiving end of such an act meant that you were under the thumb of oppression and coercion. They were often viewed as nothing more than playthings by those who took advantage of them.

The word *malakoi* was also used in reference to the "receptive" male prostitutes in pagan temples. Just like Paul's reference to same-sex behavior in Romans 1 is linked to idolatry and temple prostitution, we have the exact same context here in 1 Corinthians. *Arsenokoitai* and *malakoi* were the same-sex roles men would play in pagan temple worship. If you research the history of ancient Corinth, you will discover that the epicenter of that city was the temple to the goddess Aphrodite where people would go and offer sexual sacrifices to appease the goddess. Men would have sex with male priests or other men or men with women — every configuration you could imagine — all in an attempt to appease the deity being worshipped.

Even staunch conservative John MacArthur agrees. Describing the first-century Christians whom Paul is writing to, he says:

> They also lived in a society that was notoriously immoral, a society that, in the temple prostitution and other ways, actually glorified promiscuous sex. To have sexual relations with a prostitute was so common in Corinth that the practice came to be called "Corinthianizing." Many believers had formerly been involved in such immorality, and it was hard for them to break with the old ways and easy to fall back into them… it was also hard for them to give up their sexual immorality.[4]

With this in mind, go back and re-read those Scriptures again in 1 Corinthians 6:9-10 and 1 Timothy 1:9-11. You'll notice the same sort of context — a context that has nothing to do with love and partnership but rather coercion and force. This has nothing to do with monogamous same-sex couples as we know and understand them currently. You have to understand the context of the Bible to discern what it's talking about. Same-sex attraction and behavior were widely considered vices of excess that might tempt anyone — like gluttony or drunkenness — not the sexual orientation of a small minority of people.[1]

Arsenokoitai

But what about the other word that the NKJV translates as "sodomites"? It comes from the Greek word *arsenokoitai*, which is not a simple word to translate either because it's hardly used in the Bible. Scholars have debated whether it refers to male prostitution or pederasty (pedophilia). Other than 1 Corinthians 6:9, it only appears again in 1 Timothy 1:10.

This one word is at the heart of the debate for LGBTQ inclusion in Christianity, so we must get it right. *Arsenokoitai* is a word that the Apostle Paul made up by taking Leviticus 18 and 20's condemnation of men who lie with men as with women. It's possible he created this word from the reference in Leviticus as *arsenokoitai* (arsen = male, koites = bed), as both of those words appear together in the Greek translation of Leviticus 20:13. So he created a new word to condemn the same thing Leviticus was also condemning within his modern Greco-Roman context as well.

Once again, it seems that Paul is talking about temple prostitution, the use of sex as a worshipful sacrifice to pagan deities. There were actually 20 words in Ancient Greek that people would have known as referring to homosexuality. Yet, Paul didn't choose any of them. Instead, he appears to make up a new word — *arsenokoitai* — to refer to something unique.

Even though sexual orientation was not a concept in the ancient world, these were some of the many words for same-sex behavior that were popular at the time:

- *arrenomenes* meaning "mad" or "crazy" after men.
- *dihetaristriai* referencing lesbian sexuality and literally means love between women.
- *Erastes* (an older man who sometimes loves a younger male)
- *eromenos* (sometimes young male who loves a sometimes older man)
- *euryproktoi* (men who dress like women, also sometimes a vulgar reference to anal penetration)
- *hetairistrail* (women who are attracted to women)
- *kinaidos* (a man whose main salient feature was supposed feminine love of being penetrated by other men)
- *pathikos* (the passive penetrated partner in a homosexual couple)

I think you get the idea. My point is that if Paul had used any of these words in 1 Corinthians 6:9 or 1 Timothy 1:10, we could reasonably be sure of his meaning. But he didn't. Instead, he invented a brand new word, suggesting he had something else in mind — like rape or shrine prostitution. He is not just the only Biblical author to use this word; Paul is the only writer in all of antiquity who used the term *arsenokoitai* up to this point (that we know of). As New Testament scholar Dale Martin has written, "The only reliable way to define a word is to analyze its use in as many different contexts as possible." Martin has shown that this word's later use, after Paul's writings, referred to sexual or economic exploitation, never loving relationships.

In the 1 Timothy passage, we find the exact usage of *arsenokoitai* right beside the Greek word for "enslavers" (*andrapodistais*). So it's way more likely that this passage was meant to read "the *pias* slave boys and those who procure/enslave them."

So the word *arsenokoitai* is just condemning in Greek whatever was being condemned in Leviticus 18 and 20. To find out what Paul was talking about, you have to look at how other writers understood that word in Paul's day. And Philo, a Jewish writer during Paul's time, does tell us what this word means. He says in his book Special Laws, "In pious men as they are having received a charge in the temple there is a general indignation against those who do such things as was felt by our Law Giver." When he talks about Law Giver, he's talking about Moses, and he's saying that this word refers to pious men who work in pagan temples. So once again, we have the connection to temple prostitution.

So when Christians say, "Paul warns against the *malakoi* and *arsenokoitai*, meaning 'men who have sex with men,'" they're missing some pretty important details that completely change its modern understanding entirely.

These terms don't just refer to mere same-sex behavior — but to lustful, exploitative forms of predatory homosexual behavior. The context of Roman society suggests that Paul likely had "abusers" in mind when he condemned *arsenokoitai*. Roman and Greek males often abused younger male slaves as well as visited male prostitutes. These are unequal, abusive sexual acts, not committed and loving same-sex couples.

Commenting on Leviticus 18:22 (where it says it's an abomination for a man to lie down with another man) — Philo argues that what's being condemned is *arsenokoitai* — which, he understood to be not homosexuality, but rather shrine prostitution. That's right, in the ancient world, according to outside Biblical sources — Leviticus 18:22 isn't about being gay. Instead, *Arsenokoitai* referred to a particular grotesque version of prostitution. The same thing goes for 1 Corinthians 6:9 and 1 Timothy 1:10 — which, not surprisingly, fits the context of both of these passages, which has a lot to do with force, coercion, and lording over others.

> Paul is saying it's wrong for men to rape little boys and force them to be your sex slave.

As far as Paul was concerned, it was wrong for men to engage in prostitution (*arsenokoitai*) with effeminate, prepubescent, clean-shaven boys (*malakois*), many of whom worked as male temple prostitutes. Paul is saying it's wrong for men to rape little boys and force them to be your sex slave (shocking, right?).

So now I ask you: Is this the situation that's up for debate today regarding LBGTQ inclusion? Are same-sex couples clamoring to have the right to coercively engage in sexual acts with unwilling partners? Are they hell-bent on garnering the legal right to practice pedophilia? Absolutely not. We are not comparing apples to apples here.

"Homosexual" Never Appeared in the Bible Until 1946

Today's modern concept of homosexuality is listed nowhere in Scripture, nor does Jesus even talk about it. The word "homosexual" wasn't even invented until the 1940s. That word was inserted into the English Bible's RSV translation for the very first time in 1946.

There's actually a documentary about this that (at the time of this writing) is being produced entitled *1946: The Mistranslation that Shifted a Culture*. This new documentary investigates how the word "homosexual" was entered into the Bible, how one man tried to stop it, and how a team of researchers recently unearthed evidence that challenges deeply-held beliefs about LGBTQ+ people and their place in God's kingdom.

The creator of the documentary said, "I went into this research wanting an answer no matter what it revealed. If God said you are such a horrible abomination that I needed to rid this planet of myself, I was willing to do that because I loved God that much. But when I dug in, that's not what I found."

The first time the word "homosexual" appeared in any bible was in the Revised Standard Version (RSV) published in February 11, 1946. In the RSV's translation of 1 Corinthians 6:9, the word "homosexual" was used in lieu of the Greek words "*malakoi*" and "*arsenokoitai*." Researchers agree today these words translate loosely to "effeminacy," and "pervert," or "sexual pervert." The RSV committee voted on the decision to use the word "homosexual" instead of the accurate translations. 1946 explores how this mistranslation ignited the anti-gay movement within American conservative Christians.[5]

Kathy Baldock and Ed Oxford have dedicated their lives to researching the roots of anti-gay theology. As part of their extensive research, they uncovered 90 boxes of notes from the archives at Yale University. Filed in these boxes for over five decades was a letter sent to the RSV translation committee, written by a young seminarian named David S.

In the letter, David points out the dangerous implications that could come with the mistranslation and misuse of the word "homosexual." He believed they chose the wrong word when they put the English word "homosexual" in there.

He wrote,

> I write this after many months of serious thought and hard work to point out that which to me is a serious weakness of translation. Misinformed and misguided people may use the RSV translation of 1 Corinthians 6:9-10 as a sacred weapon.

Dr. Luther Weigle, the head of the translation committee, wrote a letter back to David S. to acknowledge their mistake and commit to correcting their grave error. But, unfortunately, the domino had already been tipped. The RSV translation went into print as-is. A later revised version of the RSV that replaced "homosexual" with "sexual perverts" wasn't published until 1971 — 25 years after the original mistranslation. By then, other translations of the Bible had applied the RSV's use of "homosexual" in biblical texts.

This one mistranslation within our modern English Bibles has wreaked havoc and damage and politicized the body of Christ ever since.

And that word "homosexual" followed through to the other mainline Bible translations that we have today. This one mistranslation within our modern English Bibles has wreaked havoc and damage and politicized the body of Christ ever since.

As the creators of the documentary mention: "Sadly, this has become the foundation for much of the anti-gay culture that exists today, especially in religious spaces. Many conservative religious leaders have used these biblical texts to condemn and marginalize LGBTQ+ Christians. And society at large has been shaped — at least in part — to believe the idea that sexual and gender minorities must choose between their faith and their identity."

Rather than acknowledging these translation mistakes and listening to other perspectives on how these Scriptures should be interpreted, the Church has doubled down on this issue because they've so politicized it.

No Ancient Concept of Sexual Orientation

From these six passages in the Bible that seem to speak to homosexual behavior, it's worth noting that our modern-day understanding of homosexuality appears nowhere in the text. To translate *malakoi* or *arsenokoitai* as "homosexual" is problematic for two reasons: it is unlikely that Paul had any concept of sexual orientation and he was certainly not describing a committed adult relationship.

The Bible does not oppose homosexuality because it does not speak of true or innate homosexuality but rather of same-sex acts by people who are not homosexuals. I can't overstate it enough. In the biblical world, the primary forms of same-sex behavior were pederasty (sex between men and adolescent boys), temple prostitution, and sex with enslaved men. Same-sex marriages between equals did not exist when the Bible was written.

As Robin Scroggs notes: "In contrast, a pervert is said to be a person who engages in acts contrary to his or her orientation. Thus a heterosexual person who engages in homosexual activity is a pervert, just as a homosexual person would be who engages in heterosexual acts."

Seward Hiltner made a similar statement: "At least in its reference to homosexuality, therefore, the Bible does not speak at all to the principal way in which homosexuality must be understood today."

It's important to note that Jesus never once explicitly discusses "homosexuality" or "homosexual marriage." And as we've seen, neither does Paul — not in the way that we, in the twenty-first century, would. How could they when those classifications weren't present during the first century?

Here's how the Oxford Classical Dictionary begins its entry on what homosexuality was and was not in classical antiquity.

> No Greek or Latin word corresponds to the modern term homosexuality, and ancient Mediterranean societies did not in practice treat homosexuality as a socially operative category of person or public life. Sexual relations between persons of the same sex certainly did occur (they are widely attested in ancient sources), but they were not systematically distinguished or conceptualized as such, much less were they thought to represent a single, homogenous phenomenon in contradistinction to sexual relations between persons of different sexes. That is because the ancients did not classify kinds of sexual desire or behavior according to the sameness or difference of the sexes of the persons who engaged in a sexual act; rather, they evaluated sexual acts according to the degree to which such acts either violated or conformed to norms of conduct deemed appropriate to individual sexual actors by reason of their gender, age, and social status…The application of "homosexuality" (and "heterosexuality") in a substantive and normative sense to sexual expression in classical antiquity is not advised.[6]

As Yale University historian, professor, and Bible scholar, John Boswell concluded:

"In sum, there is only one place in the writings which eventually become the Christian Bible where homosexual relations per se are clearly prohibited – Leviticus – and the context in which the prohibition occurred rendered it inapplicable to the Christian community, at least as moral law...the New Testament takes no demonstrable position on homosexuality." [7]

"Using the writings of the Apostle Paul outside of the original historical context in order to create any division in the body of Christ is not only anachronistic and illogical, but ethically out of line," Michael J. Distefano asserts. As Christians, we should understand this, for it is Paul himself who teaches, "*There is no longer Jew or Greek, this is no longer slave or free, there is no longer male or female; for all of you are one in Christ Jesus*" (Gal. 3:28). That isn't to say that Paul is arguing — for or against a sexual orientation — again, how could he? But he is saying that there are to be no dividing lines in the body of Christ. Full stop.

> There's not a verse in the Bible that condemns monogamous heterosexual relationships as we understand them today. The Bible is not anti-LGBTQ. It's anti-idolatry.

Paul shares a stereotypical Jewish distrust of Graeco-Roman same-sex activity but is simply not talking about loving partnerships between people with same-sex orientation. There's not a verse in the Bible that condemns monogamous homosexual relationships as we understand them today. The Bible is not anti-LGBTQ. It's anti-idolatry.

THE THREE BUCKETS
OF THE BIBLE

"There's nothing wrong with a 6th grade understanding of God... as long as you're still in the 6th grade."
- From the documentary, *The Bible Tells Me So*

When we as Christians have conversations about the topic of homosexuality, almost invariably, we always say, *"And what does the Bible say about it?"* But, as you can see from the previous chapters, the historical and contextual understanding of these six passages present a much different picture than the one most of us have been led to believe regarding the subject.

The issue of homosexuality, though, is just one piece to the greater puzzle of how the Bible should be understood and interpreted today. I know that when I was a pastor, I was reluctant to hear any perspective about the Bible other than the one that I was trained to teach — that the Bible was the inspired and inerrant Word of God without any mixture of error. So I would figuratively put my fingers into my ears whenever I thought I was encountering a different viewpoint of how the Bible could be interpreted. To be convinced of any other way other than the one I had been trained in might cause a radical and fundamental shift in my belief system. And if it didn't align with the statement of faith of my denomination, it might jeopardize my ability to keep my job. So any differing perspectives or beliefs about the Bible were literally "dangerous" to me.

On top of that, I feared that I might lose my own faith if I allowed myself to go down the rabbit hole of too many questions. But a faith that cannot be questioned cannot be trusted. I believe God wholeheartedly welcomes our questions as we discern truth. And often, those who question the most end up with a type of faith that is the strongest of all.

All of my life, I was taught that the Bible's teachings were clear when it came to the topic of homosexuality. However, once I investigated the evidence for myself, I was shocked at how something I was once so sure about wasn't the case at all. I had struggled and hated myself for nearly three decades for no reason. What else had I been wrong about? One of the sayings I used to repeatedly declare from the pulpit was "the Bible clearly says…." But the reality is, if "the Bible is clear," everyone would understand its meaning perfectly. But since everyone disagrees on what the Bible says, then apparently, it's not always clear. There are a staggering 45,000 Christian denominations globally. More are being added to that number every day simply because we cannot agree on how the Bible should be interpreted and applied today.

You have to think when you read the Bible. You're dealing with not just multiple languages where much of the meaning is lost in translation to English, but you're also dealing with cultural and historical factors that people today know little or nothing about. I'm eternally grateful for the Protestant Reformation that put the Word of God back into the hands of the people. However, the reason why the Roman Catholic Church (before the Reformation) said that common people shouldn't be reading the Bible is because it's common for the common people to get it wrong. And I'm convinced that on some topics, we usually and collectively do.

Most Christians have sadly never even read the Bible cover-to-cover. So do they really know what it says or what its true intent is? Probably not. So where do they get all of their assumptions about the Bible? Their beliefs are merely derived from what someone else tells them. How powerful of a tool (or weapon) is that?

> Most people don't really want the truth. They just want constant reassurance that what they believe is the truth.

After being a pastor for nearly 20 years, my resignation finally allowed me to be open and really question what I had always been taught to believe. I've come to the realization that most people don't really want the truth. They just want constant reassurance that what they believe is the truth. My deconstruction led to my reconstruction, and my love for God and Scripture has been renewed. My understanding of many things has shifted, but I'm enjoying seeing the peace and joy that comes when you have a holistic understanding of Scripture altogether. What I've discovered, now that I've been outside of the "pastor bubble," is that God is so much bigger than the box that evangelicals put him in, and the Bible is so much richer when you understand it within the proper perspective.

In this chapter, I'm going to first delve into many of the problematic passages of Scripture. These are some of the significant issues that have led many to walk away from the Christian faith and disregard the Bible entirely. For those who don't know me, you might assume I'm a skeptic that's attacking the Bible. Nothing could be further from the truth. But I do want you to see these roadblocks from the viewpoint of someone who would be a skeptic or an atheist and why they are so problematic if we are to maintain a "verbal plenary inspiration and inerrancy" standpoint.

Next, I want to introduce you to the Three Buckets of the Bible concept and how all biblical passages fit into one of three categories. Last, I want to share with you the implications of what a proper understanding of the Bible looks like, how to recognize both the Bible's humanity and its divine inspiration, and then studying it carefully in order to be shaped and guided by it.

Grappling with the Problematic Passages

Everyone who takes the Bible seriously knows the feeling. There are times when you'll be reading along, and you come to a passage of Scripture you're not quite sure what to do with. You think to yourself, "I don't know exactly what to do with this passage, but the plain meaning of the text doesn't seem to jive with what I know about the character of God based upon what Jesus showed us about the Father." Some statements need cultural, historical, and grammatical interpretation to make sense. But there are, on rare occasions, things that we should rightly question.

Would you like to sell your youngest daughter into slavery? Well, that's sanctioned in Exodus 21:7, but unfortunately, she'll never be allowed to be free from enslavement: *"When a man sells his daughter as a slave, she will not be freed at the end of six years as the men are."*

124

Does your next-door neighbor mow his yard and work on the Sabbath? Exodus 35:2 clearly says he should be put to death. Am I morally obligated to kill him myself, or should I call the police?

If the Biblical laws were still enforced today, many of us would qualify for the death penalty. If a man has a stubborn and rebellious son that won't listen to him or his mother, all of the men of the city shall stone him to death (Deuteronomy 21:18-21). Having premarital sexual intercourse (Deuteronomy 22:13-21), sacrificing to a god other than Yahweh (Exodus 22:20), or a child who curses his parents (Exodus 21:15,17) were all crimes punishable by death.

Then we have strange laws like the one in Deuteronomy 25:11-12 that says when men fight with one another, and the wife tries to help her husband from the person who is beating him by grabbing him by the private parts — then the woman's hand is to be chopped off! Wait a minute… she was just trying to help her husband! But now she needs her hand to be amputated as punishment? That's a peculiar law to say the least. And I don't remember ever hearing a sermon on that passage.

As we saw in an earlier chapter, a woman was also to be stoned to death if she was not a virgin on her wedding night (Deut. 22:13-21). That's something we all would say today is morally reprehensible. Yet the Bible literally gives us instructions to do it.

The Bible also says that if a man meets a woman in town and then rapes her, then the man is supposed to be stoned to death for committing the rape, but the woman is also to be stoned to death because she didn't scream loud enough for help. This is allegedly a direct commandment from God. But if the rape happens in the countryside, where no one could have heard the attack… then only the man is supposed to be stoned to death. But if she's raped in the town, it's her fault, and she must be stoned to death along with her attacker (see Deuteronomy 22:23-27). Do we really believe that it was within God's loving character to dictate that a woman raped should be killed if she didn't scream loud enough for help?

What about the issue of slavery? We have only 6 verses that deal with homosexuality. Yet, we have hundreds of verses that refer to slavery in both Testaments, none of which condemn it.

Exodus 21:20-21 says, "*When a slaveowner strikes a male or female slave with a rod and the slave dies immediately, the owner shall be punished. But if the slave survives a day or two, there is no punishment; for the slave is the owner's property.*" In other words, the Israelite was allowed to beat his slave nearly to death so long as the slave didn't die within two days of the beating.

Do we really believe this was ever God's will for human beings and how we were to live? Yet this is Scriptural law, handed down from Moses, that purports to be the command of God. How else do we explain this other than recognizing that cultural norms played a role in shaping Scriptural norms? There are things commanded in the Bible, in the name of God, that today we recognize as immoral and inconsistent with the heart of God.[1]

I would challenge every Christian to come up with a Biblical case for why slavery should be outlawed. It's really difficult to do using Scripture because slavery was completely sanctioned — even though the Israelites themselves were slaves to the Egyptians for 400 years. The reality is that the Bible says much more in support of slavery than against it. It never says that owning people is wrong. Instead, it gives explicit instructions to masters and slaves. During the Civil War, the slave-holders of the deep south clung to the Bible as evidence for why they shouldn't have to give up their slaves.

You may purchase male or female slaves from among the foreigners who live among you. You may also purchase the children of such resident foreigners, including those who have been born in your land. You may treat them as your property, passing them on to your children as a permanent inheritance. You may treat your slaves like this, but the people of Israel, your relatives, must never be treated this way."
Leviticus 25:44-46

Then in the New Testament, we have this admonition for those who are enslaved: "*Slaves, obey your earthly masters with deep respect and fear. Serve them sincerely as you would serve Christ*" (Ephesians 6:5). Even though there were slave owners in the early church, they were never commanded to let their slaves go free. Slaves were just told to obey, and Christian slave owners were to treat their slaves justly. It's almost as if the ancient people could never imagine a world without slavery. The New Testament commands slaves to return to their masters and to live in submission to them. Still, Christians working in human trafficking today do not believe that these passages relate to those caught in the web of human slavery.

For me personally, one of the most disturbing problematic passages is when we're told in the Bible that God commands the Israelites to commit mass killings of people. Genocide was a pretty regular occurrence in the Old Testament.

What would you think if our American troops went into another country and not slaughtered every man in that village? Not only that, but they would also kill every woman, every mother, and even the children — the little boys and young women who were no longer virgins. But then they would keep all of the little girls who were still virgins for themselves to be their sex slaves. Would you think that was something a holy and loving God would instruct them to do, or would your conscience tell you that was that man's idea?

Supposedly, the Israelites thought God told them to do that very thing (Numbers 31:17-18). When the Israelites were conquering the land, apparently, they didn't commit enough genocide for Moses. Moses gets angry when he finds out that the Israelite soldiers left the women and children alive. He allegedly speaks on behalf of God and commands them to go back and slaughter all of the women who had been with men but to keep all of the young virgin girls for themselves. I guess that was their reward for doing so. Is Moses really hearing the voice of God when he tells the Israelites to do this? Would we say that killing young boys, mothers of children, and keeping young girls as your sex slaves is indeed the will of God?

In Genesis, we're told that God was *"grieved to his heart"* by the violence that human beings were committing against one another, and He sends the Flood to wipe out the human race. Now God is commanding the Israelites to slaughter entire towns, tribes, and nations, showing them no mercy and providing them with no escape. How can this be?

When you read the early books of the Old Testament, the God of the universe often comes across as a tribal warlord. That's because the ancient Israelites were a tribal people, and they perceived God as a tribal deity. They saw the world and their God in tribal ways. This is how they connected with God — in their time, in their way. I do not believe for one second that God literally told the Israelites to commit genocide and bring back the virgin girls as sex slaves. But the Israelites *believed* that God wanted them to kill the Canaanites. From back to front, the Bible is the story of God told from the limited point of view of real people living at a certain time and place. The Bible looks the way it does because "God lets his children tell the story," so to speak. Speaking for Christians, capturing land and holding on to it by violence is not a gospel way of living. Christians today, therefore, have an obligation not to "follow the Bible" here and to not allow an ancient tribal description of God in the Old Testament to be the last word.

The 10 Commandments are the revolutionary moral code that many of our laws are derived from today. But it very specifically leaves out many of the vilest issues we face in modern culture today, including slavery, abuse of children, sexual assault, and genocide. I think we would all agree that those four things are more important than stealing or honoring your father and mother. I think we'd all agree that it's worse to rape someone than it is to disobey your parents. But we have to understand that the 10 Commandments were the moral code given to address the most significant issues *facing Israel* during the day and time it was written. Women, children, and slaves were viewed as man's property during that time.

Misuse of the Bible

> You can use the Bible to justify just about anything, and unfortunately, Christians have done just that throughout the ages.

You can use the Bible to justify just about anything, and unfortunately, Christians have done just that throughout the ages. The Crusaders marched into battle in Jerusalem in the name of Christ. Colonists from the Old World arrived in the New World, with Bibles and weapons in hand, to claim the Americas for Christ. We killed 56 million indigenous people over about 100 years in South, Central, and North America. Nazi German belt buckles proclaimed *"Gott Mit Uns"* — God is with us — as they sought the extermination of 6 million Jews.

For too long, the Bible has been used to support prejudice, apartheid, segregation, slavery, and second-class citizenship of women. Unfortunately, the same old trick that fundamentalists have been using throughout the ages is now being used again. Today, it's being misused to condemn gay people.

We have been conditioned to hold these beliefs by the Church. And it's unfortunate to think that the Church has historically been the place where these prejudices were born, nurtured, and promoted.

A Double Standard?

Maybe you're thinking, "Well sure, some of the Old Testament passages were troubling, but we live as New Testament Christians." Even in the New Testament, I find several passages distressing. For example:

- Teach slaves to be subject to their masters in everything (Titus 2:9).
- Women should remain silent in the churches. They are not allowed to speak but must be in submission, as the Law says (1 Corinthians 14:34).
- If a woman does not cover her head, she should have her hair cut off; and if it is a disgrace for a woman to have her hair cut or shaved off, she should cover her head (1 Corinthians 11:6).
- Everyone must submit himself to the governing authorities, for there is no authority except that which God has established. The authorities that exist have been established by God (Romans 13:1).

When he was examining that last passage, Justin Lee says that he came across a preacher who argued that civil disobedience such as sit-ins during the civil rights movement was a sin because it opposed "the authorities." But in that case, couldn't you also argue that Christians who helped the Jews escape the Nazis were violating this passage? There aren't really any Christians I know today who are arguing for a "plain sense reading" of all of these passages. I don't believe that women should have to cover their heads or stop talking as soon as they walk into church, that God approves of slavery, and I believe that Christians who fought the Nazis were heroes.

The problem with how many Christians interpret Scripture is that they have a double standard. They have no problem arguing that Paul's prohibition against women speaking in church was a cultural rule related to the issues of that day and therefore not applicable now. But as Justin Lee points out, many of the Christians who argue for a cultural interpretation of that passage would argue against the same interpretation for the passages dealing with homosexuality. [2]

> The problem with how many Christians interpret Scripture is that they have a double standard.

The Three Buckets Explained

As we read and interpret Scripture, I'd encourage you to think of three broad categories that every biblical passage fits into:

- **Bucket #1 - Those Scriptures that reflect the timeless will of God for human beings**. This would obviously incorporate everything about the story of Jesus and His teachings. For example, "Love your neighbor as you love yourself," or "forgive those who have wronged you," etc.
- **Bucket #2 - Those Scriptures that reflect God's will in a particular time but not for all time**. Everyone would agree that this would refer to much of the ritual laws of the Old Testament. The sacrifice of animals, eating pork and shellfish, etc.

- **Bucket #3 - Those Scriptures that reflect the culture and historical circumstances in which they were written but never reflected God's timeless will or character.** Such as those related to slavery, genocide, and other vile things that the Bible seems to sometimes command.

So the question regarding loving and committed relationships between same-sex people is, in which one of these three buckets do the handful of verses that speak about same-sex intimacy belong? Most conservatives on this issue say it belongs in the first bucket. Many moderates and progressives believe they fit into the second or even the third bucket.

Adam Hamilton says, "Interestingly, most conservatives I know agree that at least half of one of these Scriptures fits into the second or third bucket. Leviticus 20:13 states, '*If a man lies with a male as with a woman, both of them have committed an abomination; they shall be put to death; their blood is upon them.*' Does God really want gay men to be put to death? I don't know anyone, not even Topeka's Fred Phelps, who advocates that homosexuals be put to death. Even conservatives see this as a bucket 2 command. Progressives would put it in bucket 3, but no one today sees it as a bucket 1 command." [3]

Well, there are some exceptions. Some misguided Christians think gays should be put to death. Dr. Mel White, a gay clergyman, said, "I can't tell you how many radio stations I'm on where the opposition will say, 'Have you ever read Leviticus 20?' and I'll say, 'Yeah, I've read Leviticus 20, what does it mean to you?' He says, 'A man that sleeps with another man is an abomination and should be killed.' And I say, 'Who should do the killing, church people?'" And this presbyterian in Seattle said, 'No, that's the civil authorities' job. That's why we need to get more good men of God elected into government." And I said, 'So that they can kill us?' And he said,

"Well, you must find that hard to take Dr. White, but God said it first, and it's our job to obey." [4]

I used to be a Biblical literalist, so I know what the biggest objection would be as we consider the "Three Buckets" concept — and it's a valid concern. Maybe you're also thinking, "What keeps us from "picking and choosing" the Scriptures we like while setting aside those passages we find inconvenient or not to our liking?

My short answer to that question is simply this: *we already do*. Both conservatives and liberals regularly "pick and choose" Scriptures they want to emphasize or deemphasize, regardless of whether or not they believe in inerrancy. Everyone has ways of reinterpreting specific passages that do not support their biases and political or theological convictions.

If this idea seems unsettling to you (as it first did for me) — that Christians can set aside clear teachings of Scripture as no longer binding, seeing them as written primarily for another time and not reflecting God's timeless will — wait until you discover that this was something that the apostles and Jesus Himself did.

In Acts 15, Paul and Barnabas had been preaching to the Gentiles, and many were coming to faith in Christ. But Paul and Barnabas didn't require that these new converts be circumcised as the Law of Moses dictated, nor should they be encouraged to follow the 613 laws of the Jewish moral code. This teaching was outright scandalous to the early Jewish Christians. What right did Paul and Barnabas have to determine, on their own, that certain parts of God's law didn't apply to the Gentile Christians?

We need to be reminded that the only Scripture Paul had that he would have considered "inspired" was the Old Testament. The Law of Moses was regarded as the most important and the most authoritative. Yet Paul and Barnabas had concluded that the commands in the Law were no longer binding for those that followed Jesus. Paul and Barnabas had a meeting in Jerusalem with the other apostles along with those who opposed his teaching. What came out of that meeting was the recognition that parts of the Bible no longer reflected God's will for His people. The early church was literally "rearranging" the buckets of the Bible.

What I want you to notice is that even the apostles did not read the Bible from the perspective of "the Bible says it, I believe it, that settles it." They were willing to debate how their Scriptures applied to new situations. They recognized that parts of the Bible needed to be reinterpreted. They concluded that certain things within Judaism did not encompass God's timeless will for all humanity.

The Bible's Humanity and Divinity

These passages where God seemingly commands violence and genocide stand in stark contrast to the Noah story and to Jesus' call to love our enemies. They not only trouble thinking Christians, but they also serve as fodder to the new atheist movement, which asserts (sometimes rightly) that religion is the source of much violence in the world today.

These Scriptures used to trouble me as a pastor trying to uphold the infallibility or inerrancy of the Bible. But when I let go and just allow the Bible to have its humanity, only then did I begin to truly appreciate its divinity and inspiration.

This was something that I was never taught to do in seminary. Because my spiritual status rested on the fact that the Bible had to be completely inerrant... to not believe so would be heretical. It was an "all or nothing" proposition. So I would just ignore these passages —

like most Christians are doing today. Most people who read the Bible either don't think about these issues, gloss over these sections, or skip it altogether. As a pastor, I would only focus on teaching and living out the ones that did make sense and that I did understand.

How then should we correctly understand the Bible? First, we have to recognize the Bible's complexity and see its humanity. If we understand the Bible as having been essentially dictated by God, then, yes, we have no choice but to accept all of these troubling passages written as accurately describing God's actions, God's will, and God's character.

But if we recognize the Bible's humanity — that it was written by human beings whose understanding and experience of God was shaped by their culture, their level of consciousness, their theological assumptions, and the time in which they lived — then we might be able to say, "In this case, the biblical authors were representing what they believed about God rather than what God actually inspired them to say." If we use Jesus' words and his great commandments as a colander, we'll see that these violent passages in the Hebrew Bible contradict not only these great commands but the very life and ministry of Jesus — God's Word made flesh.

These Old Testament passages of violence and war tell us more about the people who wrote them and the times they were living in than about the God in whose name they claimed authority to do these things. Moses, Joshua, and David were Israel's heroes. These stories were written to demonstrate courage, resolve, faith, and inspire later generations still struggling with their own enemies. It's possible we can make sense of the Bible's difficult passages without having to justify every detail about them. Whenever a teaching in Scripture is at odds with the Person and Words of Jesus Christ, we are right to consider that the passage may just reflect the culture, the worldview, or the perspectives of the human author rather than the timeless heart, character, and will of God.

The Bible is the Word of God through the words of human beings, speaking in the idiom of their time. The richness of the Bible comes from the fact that we don't always take it as literally as if it had been dictated by God. We respect the Bible most when we let it be what it is and learn from it rather than combing out the tangles to make it more presentable and palatable.

> We respect the Bible most when we let it be what it is and learn from it rather than combing out the tangles to make it more presentable and palatable.

Understanding the spiral dynamics of human consciousness was one of the most enlightening insights I've ever discovered. (I'd encourage you to google "spiral dynamics" sometime when you're bored). This book isn't the place to delve deeper into that topic, but understanding this concept does bring exceptional clarity and insight. The principles of spiral dynamics show how mankind has progressed both individually and collectively through eight stages of conscious development. When you see where the consciousness of humanity was when the Old Testament was being written, how they thought of and perceived God during that time makes perfect sense. As humanity ascends in consciousness in later centuries, we also see the narrative of the New Testament becoming more expansive and inclusive as well.

When we open the Bible and read it, we are eavesdropping on an ancient spiritual journey. That journey was recorded over a thousand-year span of time, by different writers, with different personalities, at different times, under different circumstances, and for different reasons.

Revelation belonged in the New Testament. He tucked them in the back of the Bible and those four books don't even appear in his original table of contents. Still, over the course of church history, there arose a general consensus as to what books would be regarded as "inspired" writings. [6]

But how does inspiration work? Simply put, God speaks to us when we read the Bible. When we read Scriptures like the Sermon on the Mount, we feel moved, provoked, roused, stimulated, influenced, and urged to do something. Any serious student of the Bible has felt this inspiration from time to time — this sense that God wants us to do something or say something. Or how He quietly confirms and quickens a spiritual truth within our hearts.

As Hamilton says, "If this is what Paul meant, then the biblical authors were moved, urged, or compelled to write the message yet did so in their own words, with their own cultural assumptions and within the limits of their vocabulary and knowledge. They may not have communicated perfectly, but they were nevertheless used by God as they wrote. So often those who cite 2 Timothy 3:16 as the basis for their understanding of Scripture assume a view of inspiration that Paul never claimed, that Scripture nowhere teaches, and which no human being alive today claims to have experienced." [7]

Verbal, plenary inspiration is not taught in the Bible. It is not the essential meaning of "God-breathed" or "inspired" used by Paul, and it was not a doctrine taught in the creeds of the early church. It's not about having a high or low view of Scripture, but rather, in my opinion, this view is inflated and inaccurate. Some have even suggested that holding such a view of infallibility and inerrancy is a form of idolatry because you're ascribing to the Bible the very attributes and qualities that belong to God alone. Many conservative evangelicals treat the Bible as if it were the fourth person of the trinity.

> Biblical literalism is not the classical understanding of Bible interpretation. In fact, it's very modern.

Biblical literalism is not the classical understanding of Bible interpretation. In fact, it's very modern. It originates in the early part of the 20th century as a response to the growing liberalism movement that took place in the Church. So we have almost 2,000 years of Christian history without this understanding of Biblical literalism. This view of inerrancy and infallibility doesn't come from the Bible but from anxiety over protecting the Bible and regulating the faith of those who read it.

Biblical literalists are people who say they know the truth absolutely and, therefore, are entirely unable to engage in a conversation. They are only able to engage in a pronouncement. "God said it, I believe it. That settles it" is the mantra of the fundamentalist movement.

Please understand I have a lot of empathy in my heart towards Biblical literalists because I used to be one. However, now when someone says to me, "This is what the Bible says!" My response to them is, "That's what the Bible *reads*." The important thing is to understand context, language, culture, and custom that leads us to understand the meaning of what it is truly saying. We are often guilty of misreading Scripture through Western eyes.

> We are often guilty of misreading Scripture through Western eyes.

John Shelby Spong said, "Unless biblical literalism is challenged overtly in the Christian Church itself, it will kill the Christian faith. It is not just a benign nuisance that afflicts Christianity at its edges; it is a mentality that renders the Christian faith unbelievable to an increasing number of citizens around the world."

Literalism, as Susan Russell says, leads to using Bible passages as weapons. "Instead of taking the Bible literally," she says, "we should take it seriously, with deep faithfulness to the Old and New Testaments' core values of compassion, justice and peace." [8]

Our insistence on inerrancy and infallibility (something the Bible never says about itself) can become a serious challenge to one's faith in God rather than the source of faith. I believe God wants us to take the Bible seriously, but I don't believe He wants us to suppress our questions about it. I don't believe God wants us to live our lives wringing our hands over how to make the Bible behave itself, expending energy to try and make the Bible into something that it's not, and calling that "serving God." The problem isn't the Bible. The problem is coming to the Bible with expectations it's not intended to bear. When we are taught that the Bible has to meet these unrealistic expectations for our faith to be genuine, the end product is a very fragile, nervous faith.[9]

Once you make this shift in your understanding, you begin to see Scripture in such a refreshing light... and now everything begins to make sense. Nothing is in conflict. I no longer feel the pressure or need to "explain away" the problematic passages or contradictions in the Bible. Instead, I've discovered that when I come to the Bible and read it with this understanding, in true humility, rather than defending my version of it, I find God as He wants to be found.

The Arc of Scripture

Garrard Conley a gay man whose father is a Southern Baptist Pastor compares his father's beliefs to a game of Jenga – in which players take turns removing pieces from a tower of wooden blocks until the structure collapses. "All his tenets are at the bottom, and it feels very solid, but if you move one block, everything becomes unbalanced. And the one he can't move, that would bring it all down, is homosexuality, because it's all tied in to the literal interpretation of the Bible."

For many deeply committed Christians, changing their view of homosexuality feels tantamount to apostasy. Yet many of these same Christians already recognize the complexity of Scripture as it relates to these other subjects we've discussed in this chapter.

> For many deeply committed Christians, changing their view of homosexuality feels tantamount to apostasy.

My point in sharing this is not to get you to think less of the Bible... but to think appropriately and rightly about the Bible. I love the Bible because I meet God in its pages. I teach the Bible because I want to help others meet God, too. Only when we understand how we got the Bible and its historical context can we rightly apply it to our context today. And when you don't have a proper understanding of how the Bible was written and how it is to be interpreted today, you will unintentionally use it to malign whole demographics of people. If we take the Bible's humanity seriously — we find the possibility that its violence and troubling commandments are a reflection of the values and the theological and moral vision of some of its human authors, not of the God they sought to serve. They serve as a reminder to us of how easily we might be led to invoke God's name as a justification for wrong-doing in our world today.

The arc of Scripture points toward inclusion, not exclusion. The more the Bible progresses, the more inclusive it becomes. In the Old Testament, those who were sexually different—like eunuchs and barren women—were barred from entering the assembly of the Lord (see Deuteronomy 23:1). But within the progress of the Scriptural text, we see greater inclusion of gender and sexual minorities: one of the first Gentile converts to Christianity was an Ethiopian eunuch (see Acts 8:26-39). The New Testament's trajectory toward greater inclusion of eunuchs offers an important precedent for the inclusion of gender and sexual minorities today.[10]

Adam Hamilton concludes, "If every word in the Bible was virtually dictated by God, as suggested by those who hold to verbal, plenary inspiration, it would seem clear that God finds homosexual to be in the words of the Law, an 'abomination' and in the words of Paul, a 'degrading,' 'unnatural,' 'shameless act' worthy of divine punishment. Though I reject this concept of inspiration, I believe that even those who hold this view have grounds for rethinking the church's traditional interpretation of the biblical passages related to same-sex intimacy." [11]

Jesus: The Focal Point of the Bible

Today I believe that the focal point of the Bible, God's revelation to us, is all about Jesus. It seems as though most evangelical Christians have made a god out of the Bible and treated it as such. It is not the fourth person of the trinity. I believe that the only inerrant, infallible literal translation of the word of God is the incarnation of Jesus Christ. I am proposing that we hear, examine, and interpret all Scripture through the lens and filter of the definitive and unmitigated Word of God, Jesus Christ. We judge all other words of Scripture in the light of God's Living Word, Jesus.

> I believe that the only inerrant, infallible literal translation of the word of God is the incarnation of Jesus Christ.

We must always ask, "What is the heart, character, and will of God that Jesus reveals?" Even though Leviticus 21:9 commands us that a prostitute must be burned to death, Jesus befriends prostitutes and shows them mercy. These are two very different pictures of God and how God looks at the prostitute. Whenever we see a disparity between Jesus and anything else in Scripture, it's the witness of Jesus we must hold on to.

As Martin Luther said, the Bible is "the cradle that holds Christ." The point of the Bible is to point us towards Him. The Gospels are the canon within the canon. The closer a text of the Bible is to that story or to the heart of that story's message, the more authority it has. The further away it is, the less it has authority. Jesus taught us to love our neighbors, turn the other cheek, forgive those who wrong us, and pray for those who persecute us. This Living Word stands in direct opposition to the encouragement of slaughtering others or maligning entire demographics of people, all in the name of the Lord.

THE LOVE STORY OF
DAVID AND JONATHAN

"The modern idea of sexual orientation didn't exist in Biblical times, but the powerful love story of Jonathan and David in 1 and 2 Samuel suggests that same-sex couples are affirmed and blessed by God."
- Kittredge Cherry

It may surprise you that in the heart of the Old Testament is a story that appears to be about same-sex love. We've been taught to believe that David and Jonathan merely shared a "brotherly love" between one another, but there is evidence to support the idea that it may have been more than that. Many Jewish sects interpret these Bible characters differently as well. Scripture devotes more chapters to their incredible love story than any other human love story in the Bible (Song of Solomon being the only exception). The same words used to describe their relationship are the very same words used to describe intimate opposite-sex relationships. Both of these Biblical figures do not fit society's erroneous homosexual trope of weakness and inferiority. David eventually became the mighty King of Israel and the slayer of Goliath, no less. Jonathan was a noted military general who defeated the Philistines in war. Yet the love that these two men shared is worth noting.

Were David and Jonathan lovers? One can't know for sure. It doesn't refer explicitly to a physical relationship between the two men beyond hugging and kissing one another (surprising to us but not that unusual in ancient times). But it is definitely speculative given how all of the Biblical passages in the books of 1 and 2 Samuel that portray David and Jonathan's relationship are emotionally charged and highly intimate. There are many reasons why their relationship was speculated by many:

First, Jonathan is said to have loved David as his own soul and had given him his most precious possessions. 1 Samuel 18:1-4 says, *"Now when he had finished speaking to Saul, the soul of Jonathan was knit to the soul of David, and Jonathan loved him as his own soul. Saul took him that day, and would not let him go home to his father's house anymore. Then Jonathan and David made a covenant, because he loved him as his own soul. And Jonathan took off the robe that was on him and gave it to David, with his armor, even to his sword and his bow and his belt."*

Jonathan loved David, and so they consistently made time together. When they were alone, they affirmed their love for each other. Each time they reaffirm their covenant, their love for one another is the reason we are given in Scripture.

Since people in those days did not wear underwear, Jonathan stripped himself naked in front of David. That would be considered highly unusual behavior (then and now) unless their relationship was sexual in nature.

Now, imagine if this story had been about Jonathan and a woman. Suppose the author had written that "Jonathan's soul was bound to Miriam, and Jonathan loved her as his own soul." And suppose that after meeting Miriam for the first time, Jonathan immediately gave her all his most prized precious possessions. If this Scripture had been about Jonathan's encounter with a woman, theologians everywhere would be writing about this being one of the greatest love stories of all time. But because the object of Jonathan's love is a man, our cultural prejudice kicks in, and we insist they couldn't have been anything other than just really good buddies.

> If this story had been about Jonathan's encounter with a woman, theologians everywhere would be writing about this being one of the greatest love stories of all time.

Jeff Miner and John Tyler Connoley write:

> When was the last time you saw a heterosexual man, swept away by brotherly love, strip naked in front of him and offer another man his most precious possessions? Suppose the pastor of your church, upon meeting another man for the first time, stripped himself of his suit and gave it to the other. Suppose in that same encounter he also offered his most precious possessions — perhaps a family Bible, a wristwatch with an inscription from his parents, and his beloved four-wheel-drive pickup truck. Wouldn't this strike you as more than just a little "queer"? Let's face it, the author of 1 Samuel is describing a classic love-at-first-sight encounter that happens to involve two men.[1]

Even as a child hearing this in Sunday School, I remember thinking that this story sounded just a little bit suspicious. And I, too, was envious of their relationship. I secretly hoped that someday I could have that "David and Jonathan" type of relationship as well.

David and Jonathan became so close that it looked like they would someday rule Israel together. However, there was a significant obstacle looming before them. Jonathan's father, King Saul, was jealous of David as he watched his popularity in Israel grow. King Saul thought that David's rise in fame was a threat to his own rule, so he began making plans to have him killed. Jonathan makes a covenant of love and protection between him and David.

1 Samuel 20:17 says, "*Now Jonathan again caused David to vow, because he loved him; for he loved him as he loved his own soul.*" When you look at the word used here for "love," it means an immediate bond in body, soul, and spirit. Many Biblical translators translate this as saying "souls," but this Hebrew word includes the body. The implication is that both their souls and their flesh were in union. They made vows to one another twice in Scripture as one soul and one flesh. Keep in mind that the exact same wedding vows that David used for Jonathan in this situation are used in marriages all the time.

In 1 Samuel 20:41-42, Scripture says that these two men kissed each other until "*David exceeded.*" Regardless of how this phrase is translated in English Bibles, the original Hebrew text says they kissed each other and wept together until David "became large." The Hebrew word for "exceeded" is *higdil* which means "to grow." Are we to assume that David grew taller? The word *higdil* used here is the causative conjugation of the root *gadal*, meaning that David was "caused to become big." Some theologians interpret "*gadal*" in this verse as indicating that David had an erection. However, the thoughts of David becoming sexually aroused after kissing Jonathan may have been too threatening for Bible translators. They either deleted the ending entirely or created one of their own. Still, some have speculated that something sexual may have happened simply because, in the very next verse, they swear on their seed and make a covenant together.

Jonathan's father, King Saul, was angry at the vows his son had made to David. As a result, they were forced to only meet in secret. Even though Jonathan begged David to come back to the palace, David was too afraid for his life. So they made a plan. Jonathan would return home to the palace and figure out what his father was thinking. If his father had cooled down, he would let David know it was safe to return.

On that night at the royal table, Jonathan spoke up for David. But, unfortunately, he had to withstand his father's visceral reaction:

> *"You son of a perverse, rebellious woman! Do I not know that you have chosen [David] the son of Jesse to your own shame and to the shame of your mother's nakedness? For as long as the son of Jesse lives upon the earth, neither you nor your kingdom shall be established."* (1 Samuel 20:30)

Many gay men have experienced dinner conversations with their father that sounded very similar to that one. Something about his sexuality comes up. The blame goes to Mom for being "too soft" or "too harsh" or who "perverted" her son somehow. Then Dad turns his anger towards his son: "Can't you see how you're shaming the whole family? Don't you know what this will do to your career? You'll never amount to anything until you stop this."

But in the Biblical text, there's an interesting reference here that 99.9% of all readers will miss. Saul's reference to Jonathan shaming his mother's nakedness carries with it a sexual connotation. It was a euphemism used in ancient days to refer to bringing sexual shame onto the family. This phrase was used as an insult to women who had their virginity taken before marriage, which is additional proof that "uncover one's mother's nakedness" is a sexual euphemism. It's also the same phrase used in reference to Noah and Ham. Uncovering one's father's nakedness was a euphemism of a masculine male (meaning you were masculine in the act of sex), while "uncovering your mother's nakedness" was the opposite (you were feminine in the act and therefore the one being penetrated). So it's inferred that when Saul says you're uncovering your mother's nakedness, he's accusing Jonathan of being the receptive partner in sexual acts with David. Again, this was meant to be an insult to Jonathan. It appears as though Saul is actually accusing his son of having a sexually romantic relationship with David in this text.

Jonathan immediately runs to see David and tells him the terrible news. We then find their last moments together that the Bible records:

> *"David rose from beside the stone heap and prostrated himself with his face to the ground. He bowed three times and they kissed each other and wept with each other; David wept the more. Then Jonathan said to David, 'Go in peace, since both of us have sworn in the name of the Lord, saying, "The Lord shall be between me and you, and between my descendants and your descendants, forever."' He got up and left; and Jonathan went into the city."* (1 Samuel 20:41-42)

This would be the last time they would see each other. Perhaps they had some idea this was the end. They certainly knew their love was doomed. Jonathan (along with Saul) would eventually be killed in battle. Yet, in this moving exchange with one another, Jonathan reminded David of the covenant they had made between them. He reminded him that even if they could not be together, they had made a pledge to each other and that their bond between them would last through all generations.

Even when David eventually became King, he adopted Jonathan's son into his own family as his own son (which was a political move unheard of in the ancient world as the new King was expected to kill any family member with any connection to a previous, rival king).

The last reason their relationship was speculative has been referred to by many as "the smoking gun." In the first chapter of 2 Samuel, David writes a song, dedicating it to Jonathan after his death. In that song, he included these words: *"Greatly beloved were you to me; your love to me was wonderful, surpassing the love of women"* (2 Samuel 1:26).

> David acknowledged that his love with Jonathan was greater than anything he had ever experienced with a female.

David acknowledged that his love with Jonathan was greater than anything he had ever experienced with a female. Have you ever heard a heterosexual man say that he loved his friend more than he loved his own wife? Do you see now why it seems, at least on the surface, that their relationship goes much deeper than just being friends?

According to *Strong's Dictionary*, the word that David used for "love" (*ahava*) means "to have affection, sexually or otherwise, to be intimate with." It's rendered in such a way as to denote a deep longing for or breathing for another individual. *Ahava* is both a noun and a verb. It is an act that you do. It matches the word he used for the love he had for women in this same passage.

I bring this up because if the legendary King David had a same-gender relationship that was portrayed positively in the Bible, it could provide precedent for similar relationships today. It provides a picture of two men who enjoyed something that appears to be more than just a normal, everyday friendship.

In this story, we have a direct biblical answer to our question: Can two people of the same sex live in a loving, committed relationship with God's favor? The answer is "yes," because Jonathan and David did, and the Bible celebrates their relationship. The author feels no need to explain away the love between these two men, putting in a note saying, "this may look like a love story, but no hanky-panky happened." When King Saul assumes the relationship is much more than friendship, the author leaves Saul's comments in and lets the reader assume the same. The author also would have been aware of this story's similarity to other ancient near-eastern stories that contained homoerotic aspects. (Epic of Gilgamesh written in 2100 BC) He would have known that readers of his time would interpret his story with these other accounts in mind. Yet, he did not bother to differentiate Jonathan and David's relationship.[2]

The modern idea of sexual orientation didn't exist in Biblical times. Still, the powerful love story of Jonathan and David suggests that same-sex couples can be affirmed and blessed by God. To me, it's humorous how far we will go to excuse the story of Jonathan and David as mere friends when clearly there is so much more going on here. Tom Horner, in his book, *Jonathan Loved David*, said, "There can be little doubt, except on the part of those who absolutely refuse to believe it, that a homosexual relationship existed between David and Jonathan." [3]

My theological belief is that all loving relationships are honored by God. The Bible is a book about love. It's about the human condition. It's about inclusion. Remember that David was a *"man after God's own heart"* (1 Samuel 13:14), and yet his "soul was knit together" with that of another man. He is one of Israel's famous kings. He authored most of the Book of Psalms. He is in the lineage of Jesus Christ. And the Bible says that he loved a man named Jonathan...*more than he loved women.*

EX-GAYS AND CONVERSION THERAPY

"It took years of personal reflection and growth, finding forgiveness toward my family, and learning to love myself again to overcome the damages caused by this so-called 'therapy.'"
— Luke Romesberg

In an episode from the first season of the controversial animated series South Park, young Stan discovers that his dog Sparky is gay and decides he just needs good training.

"Sit, Sparky," he commands. The dog sits.

"Good boy. Now shake." The dog lifts his paw, and Stan shakes it.

"Good boy. Now… don't be gay. Don't be gay, Spark; don't be gay!"

Sparky only cocks his head, confused.

"Did it work?" Stan's friend Kyle asks.

The punchline goes to wisecracking Cartman: "He still looks pretty gay to me." [1]

In his book, *Torn: Rescuing the Gospel from the Gays vs. Christians Debate*, Justin Lee remarked that as he opened up about his homosexual struggles to the Church, he started feeling a lot like Sparky. "When many Christians found out I was gay, their only response was to shout uselessly, "Don't be gay! Don't be gay, Justin; don't be gay!"

Yes, but I am gay. So what do I do now?

"Don't be gay!"

But how? What if those programs don't work? What if God doesn't change me? What if I'm like this for a really long time, or forever? How do I live my life today, as a gay Christian who wants to follow Jesus?"

"Don't be gay!"

What is Conversion Therapy?

Conversion therapy is the practice that says LGBTQ people can heal their sexuality or gender identity and become heterosexual or cisgender through a process of pseudo-psychology and spirituality. This practice is rooted in conservative Christian theology that asserts that being gay is a sin and, therefore God should heal LGBTQ people of our brokenness. Every major psychological and psychiatric organization has said that conversion therapy is not only illegitimate but is objectively harmful. Still, that doesn't stop the Church from trying to "free people from this sin."

> Every major psychological and psychiatric organization has said that conversion therapy is not only illegitimate but is objectively harmful.

For decades, many churches promoted "ex-gay" ministries (also known as conversion therapy or reparative therapy) as a response to

LGBTQ people. This approach was based on the belief that people could essentially choose not to be gay if they worked hard enough or prayed hard enough. Ex-gays are Christians who believe God has cured them of homosexuality.

To date, 698,000 Americans have undergone conversion therapy, and out of that number, 350,000 of them were adolescents (Williams Institute, UCLA). Gay conversion therapy is still legal in 41 states. The methods are cruel and frequently violent, from applying electric shocks while being forced to watch gay porn, to mind control games aimed at persuading LGBT "patients" their desires are rooted in dysfunctional or "disempowering" relationships with their mothers.[2]

Before 1973, when the American Psychiatric Associate removed homosexuality from its official list of mental disorders, gay people were treated with various methodologies, including electroshock treatment, psychotherapy, hormone therapy, and aversion therapy. None of those methods proved successful and were outlawed as a form of treatment after 1973. However, the Church quickly picked up the mantle in helping men and women with unwanted same-sex attraction rid themselves through spiritual-based reparative therapy. Some even resort to performing exorcisms on gay men and women, believing that demons are the cause for their desires.

Born as a pastor's kid in a Southern Baptist family, Garrard Conley was sent for conversion therapy to "treat" his sexual identity. He wrote a book about his experience that was later turned into a movie entitled *Boy Erased* (starring Russell Crowe as Conley's father and Nicole Kidman as his mother). In his book, he talks in detail about the methodologies and tactics used by a Christian conversion therapy organization based in Memphis known as *Love in Action*.

The *Love in Action* conversion therapy notebook included a series of rules and prohibitions designed to maximize their mind control over patients during their treatment. Rules included restrictions on where residents could travel within Memphis, on how they dressed and groomed themselves (no "muscle shirts," no sideburns "below the top of the ear") and how they engaged with the secular world (no listening to Beethoven or Bach, or entering "non-Christians bookshops," for example). Women were forbidden to wear "mannish/boyish" clothes, and men had to avoid "campy" behavior. The handbook was analyzed by a team of experts to see whether it matched what they knew about cults…and it did.[3]

When I was a pastor preaching my sermons against homosexuality, one of the things I found great satisfaction in was finding people who were once gay and had become straight. "See here, there's proof that the gospel can change anybody! Even their sexual orientation." Hearing those stories gave me hope that I had changed too.

At one time, while pastoring in Miami, I even paraded a couple on stage who had each lived a gay/lesbian lifestyle respectively, heard the gospel and converted, went through conversion therapy, and were now married to each other. Interestingly, years later, I discovered that this couple is no longer married. I can only speculate as to why.

What's the harm in trying?

Some still say, "Maybe these conversion therapy programs don't work for everyone… but what's the harm in trying?" It turns out there's a lot of harm that can be done. A 2018 study on conversion therapy found that LGBTQ youth whose parents tried to change their sexual orientation were more than twice as likely to attempt suicide as LGBTQ youth whose parents did not try to change their orientation. LGBTQ youth were almost three times as likely to attempt suicide when sent to therapists, pastors, or religious leaders who sought to change their orientation.

The American Medical Association, The American Psychiatric Association, The American Psychological Association, The American Psychoanalytic Association, The American Academy of Pediatrics, and the National Association of Social Workers have all stated that homosexuality should not be treated as a mental disorder and that they oppose attempts at reparative conversion therapy. And that sexual orientation is not a choice and therefore cannot be changed. LGBTQ conversion practice is now a breach of professional ethics for registered health practitioners.

LGBTQ youth whose parents tried to change their sexual orientation were more than twice as likely to attempt suicide.

As reported by an American Psychological Association task force, people who have gone through conversion therapy face 8.9 times the rates of suicidal ideation, 5.9 times higher rates of depression and are three times as likely as their peers to engage in the use of illegal substances and risky sexual behaviors. These statistics simply cannot be ignored.

People who have undergone conversion activities have suffered:
- major anxiety and depression, including suicidality
- difficulties forming and maintaining relationships
- difficulty with sexual function
- guilt, shame, and grief
- deep spiritual harm at being rejected by their families, communities or losing their faith
- financial impact from costs of 'conversion' practices, lost earnings and opportunities, and later recovery
- significant delays in pursuing a career or vocation[4]

Religious fundamentalists will tell you that they know many people who have come through "Love Won Out" or reparative therapy and that they have stopped being homosexual. And yes, by instilling fear and shame into a person, you can get them to suppress any feelings that they have. However, that's a world away from changing someone's sexual orientation.

I learned while in therapy that if you suppress that part of yourself, it's not without consequences. And usually, the consequences are very serious. Your sexual orientation is at the root of who you are. Repressing your sexuality has been shown to cause severe psychological and emotional damage.

Sigmund Freud said, "Unexpressed emotions will never die. They are buried alive and will come forth later in uglier ways." Suppressing or repressing your sexuality is never a good idea. It's like trying to keep a bunch of beach balls down below the surface of the water. Sure, you can succeed at it for a little while, but when you least expect it, it's going to shoot up through the water and into the air. Michael Singer once said, "If you are resisting something, you are feeding it. Any energy you fight, you are feeding. If you are pushing something away, you are inviting it to stay." What we resist persists.

The *Journal of Counseling Psychology* released a significant study in March of 2014. After researching more than 1,600 men and women, they found sexual orientation change efforts to be completely ineffective (Throckmorton, 2014). So why does ex-gay seemingly work for some and not others? I know of no males who claim that their sexual orientation changed, though some remain married and others remain intermittently celibate…at least for a time. Married ex-gay personal friends have confided significant difficulties in their relationships due to their mixed-orientation marriages.[5]

Justin Lee says, "I could share hundreds and hundreds of stories of people who poured their hearts into ex-gay programs, prayer, and other types of therapy, only to discover that neither they nor the others in their programs ever became straight…Yes, some people have claimed that they went from gay to straight, but many of them later admitted this wasn't true, and there's a lot of motivation for people to claim a change that isn't actually happening. In those cases, even those who have married a member of the opposite sex will admit that they haven't actually gone from gay to straight, that even if they never act on their feelings, they remain unfulfilled still feeling attracted to the same sex.

Survivors of Conversion Therapy

What I had found from the "ex-gays" that I had talked to was that they often secretly struggled with severe depression. Furthermore, they had developed a pattern of living out their Christian behavior for a season, then going back out into the "gay world" again, only to return to the safety of the church, rinse and repeat. They were a confused mess to say the least.

Even these so-called "ex-gay ministries" don't claim to change a person's inner sexual desires…just his or her sexual conduct. So if these conversion therapy ministries really did work, why don't they all use the same technique? Why does each ministry experiment in its own way? And why have so many members and leaders of these ministries recanted earlier claims that they were changed?

In 2013, I remembered watching *Exodus International* apologize to the public and close its doors. As a pastor still struggling with same-sex attraction, I felt shocked and a little devastated. I remember thinking, "There really isn't any hope for gay people in overcoming this. If the world's largest ex-gay organization spanning 30 years has given up and said in effect, 'This doesn't work,' then what hope do I have of changing my sexual orientation?"

Alan Chambers, former President of *Exodus International*, admitted that 99.9% of people he knew had failed to change their sexual orientation. In recent years, Chambers has been even more absolute, saying in a 2019 interview, "No one changes their orientation; it doesn't happen." Many other former "ex-gay" leaders, from Michael Bussee to John Paulk to John Smid, have also now renounced the ex-gay movement and are now LGBTQ-affirming.

> "No one changes their orientation; it doesn't happen."
> -Alan Chambers

Restoration Path (formerly known as *Love in Action*) was another large ex-gay ministry. Among the first to raise the alarm about its methods was founding member John Evans, who left in 1975 after a friend, distraught by his failure to convert to straight, killed himself. "They're destroying people's lives," he told the Wall Street Journal in 1993. "If you don't do their thing, you're not of God, you'll go to hell. They're living in a fantasy world."

John Smid, former executive director of LIA and a gay man and Christian who would eventually admit that he'd "never met a man who experienced a change from homosexual to heterosexual". Today Smid lives in Paris, Texas, in a same-sex marriage.

The founder of one of the US's most significant conversion therapy programs, McKrae Game, came out as gay recently and apologized for harming generations of people.

After struggling to suppress his own homosexuality, Game founded *Truth Ministry* in 1999, in Spartanburg, South Carolina, rebranding it in 2013 as *Hope for Wholeness*. The organization operated in at least 15 states.

"I was a religious zealot that hurt people," he told the Charleston-based Post and Courier newspaper.[6]

One documentary that every Christian should watch is the Netflix film, *Pray Away*. As someone who intensely prayed that God would "take the gay away" for most of my life, this film truly hit home. It chronicles the life stories of men and women who sought help from gay conversion ministries and the harm that was done to them as a result. However, what impacted me the most from that documentary was hearing former leaders of these organizations share their remorse for what they used to do and teach.

In *Pray Away*, one of those former leaders said, "During my leadership time at Exodus International, I would see people fall back into homosexuality. My initial response was anger, betrayal, grief. But inside... deep inside... I was jealous."

Out of the ashes of Exodus, new ex-gay ministry networks rose up, and in the words of this former Exodus leader, "They need to stop."
He said, "There's a part of me that just wants to say, 'I'm sorry, I'm sorry, I'm so sorry.' I look back at what I used to say and teach and my response—and you know, I had a gay person tell me, 'I will never forgive you.' And I responded, 'I totally understand because I don't know if I can forgive myself.'" [7]

That says something when the leaders of all of these former ex-gay ministries throw in the proverbial towel, give up, and admit, "this doesn't work." The harm of conversion therapy efforts is why many former "ex-gay" leaders have not only renounced their former beliefs but apologized to the LGBTQ community for the damage they have caused.

Stew Baker (@stewdabaker1 on TikTok) said, "For five years, I attended an ex-gay ministry. By the time I was done with it, I was left more broken, more depressed, and filled with more self-hatred than when I entered. During this time, I was pushed out of my church and pushed out of my house I was living in. And although I was abandoned by imperfect people, I was never abandoned by a perfect God. I'm still on the road reconciling my faith and my orientation but I know God is with me every step of the way."

Don't fix what isn't broken

James Dobson of *Focus on the Family* says that if your child tells you that he or she is gay or lesbian, you should not accept them and love them for who they are, but that you should get them to change. In light of everything we now know, that's horrible advice. It's the exact opposite of what you should do. Such parenting behavior would absolutely devastate a child. It's not something that can be changed at will. To call it reparative is a misnomer because there's nothing to repair.

I've heard from many people in the ex-gay community who have now accepted themselves and their sexual orientations talk about the positive things that happened to them during their quest for healing. Many friendships were made, relationships healed, and some found a deep sense of spiritual awakening that ultimately led them down a completely different path. I believe we are personally responsible for our choices, though I realize not everyone gets to make educated ones. Like parenting, we can only do the best we can with what we know at the time. If your loved one is gay, he or she does not need "healing." We need to stop trying to fix what isn't broken.

MARRIAGE VS. CELIBACY

"Homosexuality is clearly condemned in the Bible. It undermines God's created order where he made Adam and Eve, a man and a woman, to carry out the command to fill and subdue the earth (Genesis 1:28). Homosexuality cannot fulfill that mandate." [1]
- Matt Slick

I led churches both in Miami and Kansas City in the years leading up to the Supreme Court decision that legalized marriage between same-sex couples. When the courts were starting to allow gay couples to adopt children, I hosted a press conference at my church where I spouted off my well-scripted evangelical talking points of how children need to be raised with both a mother and father and that gay couples were incapable of being parents. I was once a featured panelist on a PBS talk show representing the evangelical Christian perspective against the issue of gay marriage. Being the leader of one of the largest churches in America made me an easy target for news reporters. Whenever the topic of "gay rights" was trending, I was repeatedly interviewed by the news media more times than I can remember. Eventually, I stopped taking the requests for interviews. I was tired of talking about it. And unrelated to my own secret struggles with same-sex attraction, I began to find that my own inherited debate points on this issue really weren't holding up water within the public square. There were too many holes in my own argument about why gays shouldn't be allowed to get married.

Gay marriage was (and still is) one of the most hotly contested issues for evangelicals. Dr. James Dobson of *Focus on the Family* said, "If marriage means everything, it means absolutely nothing." Even Pope Benedict stated in January of 2012 that gay marriage threatened "the future of humanity itself." [2]

A Brief History of Gay Marriage

- The world's first legal gay marriage ceremony took place in the Netherlands on April 1, 2001, just after midnight. The four couples, one female and three male, were married in a televised ceremony officiated by the mayor of Amsterdam.[3]
- On May 17, 2004, the first legal gay marriage in the United States was performed in Cambridge, MA, between Tanya McCloskey, a massage therapist, and Marcia Kadish, an employment manager at an engineering firm.[4]
- The June 26, 2015, Obergefell v. Hodges US Supreme Court ruling made gay marriage legal in all 50 U.S. states.[5]
- By May of 2020, an estimated 293,000 American same-sex couples have married since June 26, 2015, bringing the total number of married same-sex couples to about 513,000 in the U.S.[6]

- On May 26, 2020, Costa Rica became the first Central American country to legalize same-sex marriage.[7]
- As of 2021, same-sex marriage is legally performed and recognized in 29 countries (nationwide or in some jurisdictions). Chile will allow same-sex couples to marry starting in March 2022 and Switzerland starting July 1, 2022. In contrast, 34 countries (as of 2021) have definitions of marriage in their constitutions that prevent same-sex marriage, most enacted in recent decades as a preventative measure.[8]

"God created Adam and Eve, not Adam and Steve"

Non-affirming conservatives say that from Adam and Eve in Genesis 2 to Jesus' teachings on divorce in Matthew 19, every marriage described in Scripture is heterosexual. So, therefore, same-sex marriage cannot be acceptable. William Webb has said, "The creative architecture of male and female sexuality with its part-and-counterpart configuration argues against same-sex relationships."

It's important to understand that Adam encapsulated the divine masculine and feminine forms. Eve was taken from Adam's rib. A rib isn't in and of itself feminine, so Eve had both masculine and feminine traits as well. We see this physiologically as both genders have both estrogen and testosterone present in their bodies. The existence of intersex people (those born with both working forms of male and female genitalia) contradicts the assumption that men and women can always be divided into two very separate categories. According to experts, around 1.7% of the population is born with intersex traits – comparable to the number of people born with red hair.[9] The conservative viewpoint is that God created two genders, both for each other only — male and female. However, the creation story in Genesis is full of a rhetorical device known as merisms where "a whole is alluded to by some of its parts." One can use the example of God creating day to night to further explain this idea. When Scripture says, *"There was evening, and there was morning, the first day,"* it includes dusk and dawn, late morning and early afternoon. So "evening and morning" are used to encompass all times of the day.

Another Biblical example of a merism would be "Alpha and Omega" or "beginning and end." When these phrases are used to describe God, we understand that God is not just these two things. Instead, God is all things, not just the beginning and the end but everything in between. The same argument can be made for the merism of "male and female" as it reflects the spectrum of gender.

The reality is that same-sex marriage was not on the radar screen in the ancient world, which is why the Bible never addresses it. Ephesians 5:21-33 teaches that marriage is about keeping a covenant with one's spouse to reflect God's covenant with us. Same-sex couples can live that principle out in their relationships.

Which type of "Biblical Marriage" do you prefer?

When people say, "We are in favor of Biblical marriage," we need to ask, "Which type of Biblical marriage are you referring to?" There are many different marriage arrangements found in the pages of the Bible. Here are just a few:

- **Polygamous marriage**: One of the most common forms of marriage where a man has more than one wife.
- **Levirate marriage**: When a woman was widowed without a son, it became the responsibility of the brother-in-law or a close male relative to take her in and impregnate her. If the resulting child was a son,

he would be considered the heir of her late husband (see Ruth and the story of Onan - Gen. 38:6-10).

- **A man, a woman, and her property** — a female slave: The famous "handmaiden" sketch as performed by Abraham (Gen. 16:1-6) and Jacob (Gen. 30:4-5).
- **A man, one or more wives, and some concubines**: The definition of a concubine varies from culture to culture, but they tended to be live-in mistresses. Concubines were tied to their "husband," but had a lower status than a wife. Their children were not usually heirs, so they were safe outlets for sex without risking the line of succession. To see how badly a concubine could be treated, read the horrific account of the Levite and his concubine in Judges 19:1-30.
- **A male soldier and a female prisoner of war**: Women could be taken as booty from a successful campaign and forced to become wives or concubines (Deuteronomy 21:11-14 describes the process).
- **A male rapist and his victim**: Deuteronomy 22:28-29 describes how an unmarried woman who had been raped was commanded to marry her attacker.
- **A male and female slave**: A female slave could be married to a male slave without consent, presumably to produce more slaves.
- **Monogamous, heterosexual marriage**: What you think of as the standard form of marriage, provided you think of arranged marriages as the standard. Also, remember that inter-faith or cross-ethnic marriages were forbidden for large chunks of biblical history.

We have so many different forms of "Biblical marriage" because the cultural norms changed as history progressed. The important thing to realize here is that none of these models are described as better than any other. All appear to be accepted — some are even commanded. In Bible times, marriage was about acquisition. A man acquired his wife. We don't do that anymore. Women were expected to be a virgin at the time of marriage (and lack of proof of virginity would result in stoning - Deut. 22:20-21), but the man was exempt from that requirement. Jewish tradition used to be that the man consecrated the woman by putting a ring on her finger. And she was consecrated to him. He could have other wives, but she could have no other husbands. Nowadays, we have a two-ring exchange — both are made holy to each other. The man isn't taking additional wives, and she's not taking other husbands. Furthermore, in ancient times, daughters were married off as soon as they reached child-bearing age, which was shortly after they got their first period — around the age of 12 or 13. Today we know that girls that age may physically be ready to bear children, but we know they are not emotionally mature enough. Today, what parent would think of allowing their 12-year-old daughter to get married to an older man? Things change. And just because something is written in the Bible doesn't mean that's how we do it today.

> In Bible times, marriage was about acquisition. A man acquired his wife. We don't do that anymore.

The next time someone says, "I believe we need to stick to Biblical marriage in this country," simply ask for clarification. Which one of the eight kinds of biblical marriage would you prefer?

Song of Solomon: a Celebration of Sexuality

We do have contained in Scripture an entire book that seems to celebrate sexuality. Pastors don't know what to do about Song of Solomon. Some scholars consider it an allegory of God and Israel or of Christ and the Church (very awkward to read it as such, by the

> If we were to read all of Song of Solomon, we would find that it does not appear that these two lovers are even married.

way). Yet most scholars take it more simply and consider it erotic poetry. Since Song of Solomon is attributed to Solomon, and he is notorious for his hundreds of wives — erotic poetry was probably right up his alley. If we were to read all of Song of Solomon, we would find that it does not appear that these two lovers are even married. The lovers' dream of being together, but they do not marry or even plan on marriage. There's no indication they were even engaged. The Bible gives no indication of that. The woman refers to her friends and the protection of her brothers. We find that these two lovers feel the need to meet in secret. The most literal reading of this book is that they were sneaking around having wild and enthusiastic premarital sex. In Song 8:1-2, the female wishes that her lover was her brother so that she could kiss him in public without being teased, and they could be together in the home of her mother. The woman in the book explicitly discusses how their sexual relationship was illicit and how she won't allow other people to control her. She describes her brothers trying to lock her away in a garden, which may or may not be literal but is definitely about controlling her sexuality. She is beaten in the streets by men who disapprove of her running around at night. She also unapologetically claims her own pleasure. Solomon calls her "my sister, my bride" but the word for bride is affectionate, no more literal than the word for sister. Perhaps they later get married, and she becomes one of Solomon's many wives, but that's not addressed at all in the book. By including Song of Solomon in the canon, it appears God holds our sexual relationships in high regard. However, its literal interpretation doesn't always square with the teachings of many of today's churches.

Porneia: What is "Sexual Immorality?"

Porneia is the Greek word that is often translated as *"fornication,"* *"immorality,"* or *"sexual immorality"* in our English Bibles. In a 2011 JBL article, Kyle Harper examines the usage of *porneia* from its classical uses through the New Testament and into the early church. He had hoped to specify its meaning since the English translation of "sexual immorality" is so vague that it "inevitably threatens to become little more than a cipher for the interpreter's own views."

Jonathan Poletti says,

> Growing up Evangelical Christian, this is what you often learn: You have a sinful, evil yearning, called 'lust.' It makes you want to look at naked people and touch them! Maybe have sex—but stop yourself. You have to be married! You'll be punished! It's fornication! It's bad, and you're bad for even thinking about it. 'Lust' is a thought crime…What you wouldn't know, until you get into scholarly literature, is that all of this relies on a single Greek word, porneia, often translated 'fornication'. . . and used . . . a handful of times. Oh. And nobody knows what it means.[10]

Porneia is a cornerstone of Christian sexual morality. Yet, remarkably, its meaning has remained elusive for modern interpreters. It's derived from the Greek word for "prostitute." Later, the word passed into Latin as *fornicatio* and then into English as "fornication." But the idea of fornication is effectively limited to the Church's usage hundreds of years after the Bible was written. One of the most thoughtful contemporary interpreters of Christian sexuality has warned that "the precise meaning of *porneia* is simply uncertain given the lack of evidence we have."

Back in 1972, Bible scholar Bruce Malina said that "The N.T. evidence [about the meaning of porneia] is not at all clear."

Dale B. Martin noted in 2006, the meaning is "simply uncertain given the lack of evidence we have."

It's an incredibly rare word. But from what we can tell, this word doesn't mean "fornication" and "other sexual offenses." When examining how *porneia* was used in Classical Greek, it's almost always used to refer to **the practice of selling access to one's body.** It's a substantive of the verb that means "to prostitute oneself."

In the Septuagint, the Greek translation of the Old Testament and the New Testament, we have many references to *porneia*, and they're not always sexual in nature. It could also refer to spiritual idolatry — the idea of turning away from Yahweh and prostituting or selling yourself out to some other god.

From the Wisdom of Solomon 14:12, "*For the invention of idols was the beginning of* porneia, *and the discovery of them the corruption of life.*" This word is used in conjunction with something to do with idolatry and worshipping the wrong god.

In Hebrews 12:16, Esau is discussed as a "fornicator" (*porneia*) since he "*sold his birthright for a single meal.*" That seems bizarre because there's no sex in that soup story of Genesis 25:34.

The more you follow the trails of *porneia*, the more you drop down into stories where unmarried sex isn't the problem. In 1 Corinthians 10:8, Paul says: "*We should not commit* porneia, *as some of them did — and in one day twenty-three thousand of them died.*" This is a reference to Numbers 25. During the Jewish Exodus, the Israelites stopped at a pagan city. They decided to stay there, intermarrying with the pagan women and worshipping their gods instead of Yahweh. The women are married. The problem isn't marriage itself. The problem was that the Israelites were marrying into another spiritual system.[11]

Remember that, in Jewish law, polygamy was a social norm, divorce was fine (cf. Deut 24:1–4), and concubines and harems were all seen as being morally and socially acceptable. No verse in the Bible or statement in the Mishnah or Talmud contains any specific prohibition of premarital sex.[12] Rachel Biale explains: "in biblical law a married man who has sexual relations with an unmarried woman is not guilty of any offense since he could theoretically marry that woman." She adds: "a man who had such extramarital sex, if he did not try to marry the woman, had not committed a sexual transgression." [13]

"As it turns out, most of the references to prostitution in Paul's Bible are figurative, referring to Israel's unfaithfulness to the Lord and worship of other gods, which also help explain Paul's treatment of porneia in terms of unfaithfulness to God," note Roy E. Ciampa and Brian S. Rosner.

To sum it up, Harper's research shows us that *porneia* has many strata of meaning that accrued over the centuries. It does sometimes refer to extramarital sex, but the idea of "fornication" within Christianity developed in a society where the legitimacy of sex was determined not by the presence or absence of marriage so much as the status of the woman involved. In a letter from Gregory of Nyssa, an ancient church father, we have this interpretation confirmed that the nature of a sexual sin (at least in the 4th-century church) was determined by the woman's place in society. In the ancient patriarchal society, the distinction between what constituted "adultery" or "fornication" turns on the woman's status, not the man. The dominant trend in the use of *porneia* was having sex with prostitutes. The Romans considered prostitution a social necessity, an alternative to the violation of respectable women, and therefore a solution to adultery. Paul saw marriage as the solution to the temptations of easy sex with dishonored women.[14]

Sergius and Bacchus: An Ancient Gay Couple Martyred for Their Faith in Jesus

There's actually much evidence in the early church of same-sex paired saints. For example, the right of *adelphopoiesis* or "brother-making" was an earlier version of same-sex marriage in the first centuries of the early church. In these ceremonies, two men would express their love and commitment to one another. These stories are written about in many books, including John Boswell's book on early LGBTQ saints. There are over 40 same-sex couples we know about from early church history, but Sergius and Bacchus are perhaps the most inspiring couple we have knowledge about.

Saints Sergius and Bacchus were third-century high-ranking young officers in the Roman army. Sergius was *primicerius* (commander) and Bacchus was *secundarius* (subaltern officer). The oldest record of their martyrdom describes them as *erastai* (Greek for "lovers"). These were Roman soldiers who became Christians and eventually were executed for their faith in Jesus. They were tortured to death around 303 AD in present-day Syria after they refused to attend sacrifices to Zeus because they were followers of Christ.

Sergius and Bacchus were arrested and paraded through the streets in women's clothing to mock and humiliate them as a gay couple. Early accounts say that this couple bravely responded to their mockery by chanting that they "were dressed as brides of Christ." They told their captors that women's dress never stopped women from worshipping Jesus, so it wouldn't stop them either. Then Sergius and Bacchus were separated and beaten so severely that Bacchus died.

According to early manuscripts, Bacchus appeared to Sergius that night with a face as radiant as an angel and told Sergius not to give up because they would be reunited in heaven as lovers.[15]

Author Chris Glaser describes the vision in his book "As My Own Soul: The Blessing of Same-Gender Marriage":

> "Tortured, Bacchus died but appeared to Serge in a vision in prison. Radiant, Bacchus told Serge they were "bound together" forever and would be reunited and that "your crown of justice is me, my crown of justice is you." (Crowning was a part of opposite-gender ceremonies of the time)."

Over the next few days, Sergius was tortured and eventually beheaded.

A Coptic church hagiography states that the body of Bacchus was tossed into the Euphrates River and discovered by a pair of holy men. They are described as brothers, but that is sometimes a code for a gay couple:

> "The Lord protected the body and the waves brought it to the shore near two ascetic holy men who were brothers. The angel of the Lord appeared to them and commanded them to go and carry away the body of the Saint. When they came to where the body was, they found an eagle and a lion protecting it. The beasts spent a whole day and a night guarding it without harming it, although they were beasts of prey, for they had been commanded by divine providence to protect the body. The two holy men took the body

with great honor, singing hymns until they came to their cave where they buried it."

Sergius' tomb became a famous shrine. For nearly 1,000 years, the couple was revered as the official patrons of the Byzantine army. Many early churches were named after Sergius and Bacchus. In addition, they have been recognized as martyred saints by the Catholic, Eastern Orthodox, and Oriental Orthodox churches.

Single but Celibate?

Some believe that the expression of homosexuality is sinful. But on the other hand, they would state that the tendency to homosexuality is, in and of itself, blameless.

Today, the majority of the Church asserts that if gay Christians can't marry someone of the opposite sex, then the Bible's prohibition of same-sex relationships requires them to be single and celibate for life.

It seems as though gay men and women have drawn the proverbial short straw in life. Everyone else gets to fall in love and marry who they love — just not them. Does that seem fair to you?

As Matthew Vines reminds us, the Bible teaches that celibacy is a gift, not something that should be forced upon anyone. In Genesis, God says, "*It is not good for the man to be alone*" (Genesis 2:18). In the New Testament, Jesus says celibacy can only be accepted by those to whom it is given (Matthew 19:11-12). Paul also agrees and says that while he would prefer everyone to be celibate like him if a person cannot control themselves, then they should marry "*for it is better to marry than to burn with passion*" (1 Corinthians 7:7-9).

Some make the argument to say, "Aren't straight people who never find an appropriate partner "forced" into celibacy the same way?" No. The difference is that if a straight person eventually finds a suitable partner, they're free to marry, while a gay person is not.[16]

If you think that in the first century, two men or two women marrying each other would have been anathema had it even been under consideration, you're probably right. In Bible times, divorce was also a very big deal. Yet the majority of churches today — including those who view same-sex marriage as a sin — not only accept divorced members but allow them to be church leaders. Why? Because marriage was seen as a different institution in the time of Christ and there are valid reasons for contemporary cultures to allow divorce in certain cases. Why not make the same cultural allowances for gay couples that Christian churches have long pushed for the divorced, for women, the disabled, and others who faced discrimination back then?

When the Church says to the gay community, "We now know you can't change, so just follow Jesus and be celibate," those are easy words to say — but would you want to live that kind of life? What would it be like for you, as a straight individual, to be told that to fall in love with someone of the opposite sex was strictly forbidden? That you would need to live the rest of your life in celibacy and loneliness, knowing that other people could give and receive love within the context of a committed relationship…but not you? That would be an absolutely miserable way to live. I can no longer believe that God would carve out this path for anyone. And yet that's the message that the evangelical Church has presented to the gay community.

Do a thought experiment with me for a moment. Imagine you are a married, heterosexual person who has been married for over 25 years. Imagine that your life up to this point altered in only one way, that instead of partnering with someone of the opposite sex, you had partnered with someone of the same sex. All of your shared experiences are the same. All of your loving moments are the same. All of your times of joy, even suffering, alike in every way except for one. How, then, would it be sinful—rather than loving — if the only variable is that you are sharing these experiences with someone who shares your gender or sexual orientation? How, exactly, would you be violating what Jesus calls the greatest commandment, that we are to love God and neighbor?[17]

One of the most excellent definitions for "sin" that I've ever heard is this: *anything that causes suffering.* When it comes to the arc of Scripture and the teachings of morality in the Bible, sin is when we cause suffering towards ourselves or others. It is that very suffering that God desires to protect us from. How then would two same-sex individuals who love and desire to share their lives with each other cause suffering? The only suffering being caused today is by closed-minded, religious people (albeit well-intentioned) who ostracize them and treat them as second-class citizens based on their misguided beliefs. So then I ask, who is causing the suffering? Who is committing the sin?

THE WAY FORWARD

"Go and love someone exactly as they are. And then watch how quickly they transform into the greatest, truest version of themselves. When one feels seen and appreciated in their own essence, one is instantly empowered."
— Wes Angelozzi

Closets are a place of death. No one deserves to live "in the closet" where they must hide who they are from the world. Yet, many gay people are forced to live within two different realities. The world in which they are pretending to be someone they're not, and then that "closet world" where they have all these fears and feelings of guilt, anger, and shame.

This is probably why "Don't Ask, Don't Tell" is so important to the military and to the church. They'll let you serve as a choir director, organist, worship leader, or pastor — as long as you don't tell or talk about it. But once you "do tell" — then you're cut off from all of that conversation and interplay with others that makes you emotionally healthy.

So all throughout their lives, gay people feel as if they have to carry their biggest secret on their own. They know that once that secret is "out," it will forever alter and change how people perceive them in the world.

This is why it was such a struggle for me to write this book and put my name on it. I don't want to be known first and foremost by my sexuality. I have a mission and a calling in this life, and talking about my sexuality certainly isn't it. But I also felt compelled to write this book because I could no longer sit idle watching so many in this community being hurt by religious misunderstanding. The same misunderstanding that I myself propagated during my tenure as a pastor.

In working as a life coach within the LGBTQ community, I've seen themes emerge while listening to their stories: self-loathing, depression, mental health issues, rejection by friends and families, thoughts of taking their life, and suicide attempts appeared consistently. When I was a pastor, I believed and taught that these "symptoms" were just the by-product of living a sinful lifestyle. However, these themes seem to emerge almost exclusively among gay men or women with religious and/or conservative backgrounds. LGBTQ people of faith and religion experience these things with greater intensity and have additional issues to deal with.

A review of 850 research papers concluded that people with religious involvement and belief system have better mental health outcomes. They have a higher level of psychological well-being such as life satisfaction, happiness, positive affect, higher morale, and less depression and suicide. If, however, you are gay or lesbian (in the closet or your sexuality/belief system remains unresolved)…it is the *exact opposite*. It can literally drive you insane (increase in mental health issues) or kill you (suicide). Also, it should be noted that research has shown that the very places where Christian young people should feel the safest (church, Christian homes, schools, and with friends) are actually places of emotional, mental, and spiritual harm.

The way I see it — the enemy is not closed-minded individuals, churches, religious leaders, or conversion therapy organizations. The enemy is ignorance. Change is created by focusing our energies on overcoming the latter instead of attacking the former.

> The enemy is not closed-minded individuals, churches, religious leaders, or conversion therapy organizations. The enemy is ignorance.

Colby Martin wrote:

> "I long for a day when young boys and girls don't have to hide who they are or give up on their dreams because they are gay. I long for a day when men and women don't marry the wrong gendered person, because they think they have to or because they think it will fix them, and then years later have to navigate how to (or if to) slowly dismantle a family. I long for a day when gay Christians are not seen as godless pagans who have turned their backs on their faith, their Lord, and their church." [1]

Good Fruit, Not Bad Fruit

In his book, *God and the Gay Christian*, Matthew Vines makes a valid argument that also serves as an indictment on the modern church. He says that the experience of sound Christian teaching should result in good fruit, not bad fruit.

In Matthew 7:16-20, Jesus says, *"By their fruit you will recognize them. Do people pick grapes from thorn-bushes or figs from thistles? Likewise, every good tree bears bad fruit. A good tree cannot bear bad fruit, and a bad tree cannot bear good fruit. Every tree that does not bear good fruit is cut down and thrown into the fire. Thus, by their fruit you will recognize them."*

What kind of "fruit" has the church's approach resulted in the gay community? The result is that non-affirming beliefs about same-sex relationships have contributed to devastating harm in LGBTQ people's lives. Studies from the Family Acceptance Project have shown that "lesbian, gay, and bisexual young adults who reported higher levels of family rejection during adolescence were 8.4 times more likely to report having attempted suicide, 5.9 times more likely to report high levels of depression, [and] 3.4 times more likely to use illegal drugs...compared with peers from families that reported no or low levels of family rejection."

> It's estimated that every 5 hours, an LGBTQ teen takes his or her life. And for every teen that takes their own life, there are 20 more that try.

It's estimated that every 5 hours, an LGBTQ teen takes his or her life. And for every teen that takes their own life, there are 20 more that try. They're afraid to talk to their parents, and they're afraid to speak to their peers about what they're going through. And sadly, many will resort to that irreversible decision of ending their lives. The actual toll of lives we have lost to suicide are impossible to count. I've become deeply burdened by the number of LGBTQ men and women who are now dead due to the untruth being taught by the Church.

The Trevor Project, a national hotline that ministers to LGBT teens contemplating suicide, says that out of the top five reasons teens call their hotline, the number one is for religious reasons. They feel like there isn't a place in this world for them and God. Well-intentioned Christians have become the unwitting assassins of gay people's faith.

Because of the church's teachings that homosexuality is wrong, sinful, a perversion, and abominable before God — it has created a climate in which gay, lesbian, bisexual, and transgender children grow up feeling very much in conflict with the world in which they live.

This upbringing shapes their thinking, so they grow up hating themselves. They internalize this judgment and condemnation they've heard from the pulpit as judgment and condemnation from God. They've spent their entire lives trying to "pray away the gay," but that prayer seemingly never goes answered. So they're left to feel as though God Himself hates them and has turned His back on them — allegedly destining them for conscious eternal torment in hell…all because their prayers towards Him have seemingly gone ignored.

Is it any wonder why so many gay and lesbian men and women have turned their backs on the church and closed their hearts off to God? Should we really be that surprised?

Nadia Bolz-Weber said, "People don't leave Christianity because they stop believing in the teachings of Jesus. People leave Christianity because they believe in the teachings of Jesus so much, they can't stomach being part of an institution that claims to be about that and clearly isn't."

Jesus spent most of his time with the type of people that most Christians these days don't want in their church. Read that again. One of the charges Jesus' opponents had against him was that He was a "glutton and a drunkard, a friend of tax collectors and sinners." Surely the faith He founded should never be known for looking down on anyone.

> Jesus spent most of his time with the type of people that most Christians these days don't want in their church.

Jesus never addressed the subject of homosexuality, other than what can be inferred from his example of loving and accepting everyone, especially the oppressed and those whom the religious establishment considered unclean.

All of these consequences in the LGBTQ community due to how they've been treated by the Church are "bad fruit," and they should lead us to reconsider the source of that fruit: our interpretation of Scripture.

The Tide is Shifting

For most gay men and women living in the West, the influence of education and human rights law have allowed for great changes to take place — making the journey of self-acceptance just a little bit easier. Yet, for most gay individuals, it's still a painful journey, not just for them individually but for their families as well.

We are seeing a shift in the church on this topic, but it is slow. Frustratingly slow. However, history tells us it has always been this way. Whether it be the Anti-Slavery Movement of the mid-1800s, the Women's Rights Movement of the early 1900s, or the Civil Rights Movement in the mid-1900s — the church has always been reluctant to embrace change. Whenever there's a shift in society's consciousness about equality and human rights, not only has the church usually been the last to embrace it, but they have also actively resisted and opposed that change. History informs us that Christians are often slow learners and the Church as a whole suffers from those learning disabilities. The longer churches put this issue on the back burner, the further behind they become.

As an extreme example of how some Christians can be the last to keep up with the times, I recently discovered that there's even a

Facebook group called *Christians Against Dinosaurs* because "dinosaurs are not found in the Bible." The group aims "to respect Jesus and see through the various dinosaur deceptions." One quote of a person in the group: "I'm getting sick and tired of dinosaurs being forced on our children."

This is obviously an extreme and polarizing example, but it illustrates how Christianity has been the last to accept anything new. When Galileo invented the telescope, he was ordered by the Church to turn himself in and begin trial for holding the belief that the Earth revolves around the sun, which was deemed heretical teaching by the Church at that time. The Church's rationale at the time was based on a "plain sense" reading of several passages like Psalm 104:5, *"The Lord set the earth on its foundations; it can never be moved."*

People of color were once told to go to the back of the bus. Women were once told their only place was in the home. However, the paradigm shift in understanding that happened regarding people of color and women's equality is now happening in regard to sexual orientation and gender identity.

The church has adjusted its position on slavery, divorce and remarriage, transracial marriage, and other cultural issues. If history is any indicator, and it is, it will also adjust its position on LGBTQ acceptance. The only question is how long it will take.

The reason evangelicalism fails to understand another perspective regarding the LGBTQ community is largely due to supremacism that denies the possibility of being wrong. When anyone thinks their beliefs are absolute truth and their interpretation of Scripture is the absolute standard, then by default, all others are incorrect. Therefore, they are the only ones who need to change their mind. Conversation isn't possible with people who believe they are incapable of having holes in their worldview. Evangelicals have been given a neatly packaged system of beliefs, taught to defend it, and told they're doing it right when they mistake accountability for "persecution."

As Anthony Venn-Brown says,

> If churches continue to hold on to the outdated Christian belief that homosexuality is a sin then it makes them increasingly irrelevant to those who have gay and lesbian friends, family members, and work colleagues. The previous Christian labels of unnatural, perverse, evil, and even abomination not only do not fit, they are offensive to LGBT people and their friends and family. [2]

There are typically three different types of churches when it comes to their attitudes regarding gay couples:
- Welcoming = you're welcome BUT…
- Accepting = we accept you BUT…
- Affirming = we love you FULL STOP.

Some say the price of authenticity is our belonging. While that certainly can be true, I also believe that often what we thought was belonging all along really wasn't! Belonging means you are loved, celebrated and welcomed for all of who you are. If we have to conform to someone else's ideas before we belong, then it is not true belonging. In fact, it is something to flee from. I know that there is a cost that comes with being you. Most of the things in life worth fighting for come with one. Yet the peace, the beauty, and the power of belonging far outweigh that cost. That's why I encourage my gay brothers and sisters to choose honesty and choose to be all of who God created them to be.

"I will not stay, not ever again, in a room or conversation or relationship or institution that requires me to abandon myself."
-Glennon Doyle

I resonate with the words of Glennon Doyle, who said, "I will not stay, not ever again, in a room or conversation or relationship or institution that requires me to abandon myself."

The Gay Community: A Place Where God is At Work

In our diversity and in our uniqueness, God is glorified. The condemnation that people launch against the LGBTQ community is unfounded in Scripture. God doesn't condemn LGBTQ people. He made them and loves them just as they are.

In 2011, the Pew Research Institute released a study showing that while every demographic in the United States was leaving their affiliation with Christianity, there was one community where there was a consistent uptick in their affiliation with the Church. Guess which community that was? It was the LGBTQ community.

From 2011 onward, while so many people are walking away from the Christian faith — LGBTQ people are discovering (or rediscovering) the radical message of this rabbi from Nazareth — Jesus. What I find ironic is that the institutions of the church that are now dying are the ones that are putting up walls and saying to the LGBTQ community, "You are not welcomed and affirmed here." Could you imagine Jesus turning away people who wanted to follow Him? There really is a revival happening in the Church — but it's coming from a community most people would least expect.

In Acts 10, there's a story of how Peter had his eyes opened to God's inclusive vision of mankind. Peter at first believed that the Church was only for Jewish people. But in Acts 10, God calls Peter to preach to the Gentiles. Peter preaches the gospel, and an entire Gentile family is baptized into the Church. Peter's theology at the time said, "This cannot happen! Gentiles can't be a part of this thing that Jesus started!" And yet, Peter sees the Spirit of God moving, and he changes his theology. He changes his understanding of what the Bible teaches based on his experience of Gentiles professing their faith in Jesus. If you read on, in Acts 11, Peter returns to Jerusalem and gets chastised for this by the other apostles. They say, "How can you baptize Gentiles? You know that Gentiles aren't a part of what Jesus is doing!" And Peter says, "I preach the Gospel and the Spirit of God fell. Who was I to stand in the way of God? If these people want to follow Jesus, we need to accept them." And guess what? The Scriptures say that the Apostles heard this, and they rejoiced. They accepted Gentiles into the fold of the Christian faith.

Sadly, the Christian Church is doing the exact opposite with people of faith who are also LGBTQ. God's Spirit is moving among this community — we can clearly see that from the statistics. There's a growing number of believers who are saying, "I am gay and I am Christian and that is not a contradiction." Yet there are so many churches who say in response: "You're not a real Christian and you are not following Jesus." Instead of evangelizing, the Church is pushing these people away. The Church is resisting the new thing that God is doing. The good news: the evangelical gatekeepers don't get to decide who is a part of God's Church. Jesus does.

What Eunuchs in the Bible Teaches Us

The closest idea we have to homosexual orientation in the Bible is the idea of being a eunuch. Eunuch literally means "the keepers of the bed," as the eunuchs served and guarded the women in royal palaces and wealthy households. Their employers wanted to be certain that the eunuchs would not get sexually involved with the women they were supposed to protect, so many eunuchs were either castrated men or homosexual men. However, eunuchs referred to in Genesis, Isaiah, Jeremiah, and Daniel were not all castrated males.

Eunuchs were often functionally, if not constitutionally, homosexual. The term "eunuch" included many sexual minorities that we would fit under the LGBTQ umbrella today.

Jesus speaks about three kinds of eunuchs: *"For there are eunuchs who have been so by birth, and there are eunuchs who have been made eunuchs by others, and there are eunuchs who have made themselves eunuchs for the sake of the kingdom of heaven. Let anyone accept this who can"* (Matthew 19:12). Notice that Jesus acknowledges that there are eunuchs who have been so since birth (i.e., homosexual men who were born that way). Some Christians confidently assert that God would never create homosexual people "that way." But apparently, Jesus disagrees with them. In Jewish culture (reflected in the Talmud), natural or born eunuchs were those men who had feminine characteristics or behavior (like many modern gay men) and were commonly associated with homosexual desire.[3] The implications of Jesus' statement are profound — God created these men just the way they are.

Although the Bible doesn't speak much to the sexual orientation of eunuchs, we have plenty of evidence from ancient writings that eunuchs were widely associated with homosexuality. They were uniquely regarded as being sexually interested in men, and not having any sexual interest in women. Lucian, a Greek satirist who lived about one hundred years after Christ, compares a eunuch with a concubine to a deaf man with a flute, a bald man with a comb, and a blind man with a mirror.[4] In other words, a eunuch has as much need for a woman as a fish has for a bicycle.

> Eunuchs in Bible days were widely associated with homosexuality.

Philo, a first-century Jewish philosopher, not only upheld the ban on eunuchs but associated eunuchs with male homosexual prostitutes.

Alexander the Great's palace had "herds of eunuchs, also accustomed to prostitute themselves [like women]." [5] Quintus Curtius also reports that Alexander the Great fell deeply in love with a eunuch named Bagoas, and they entered into a relationship of mutual love.

There is some evidence to suggest that in the days of antiquity, eunuchs (gay men) were thought to have mirrored in themselves the divine union of maleness and femaleness that is traditionally thought to be the image of the Creator. After all, the image of the Creator is male and female, according to Genesis 1:27. Straight people, who lack either masculinity or femininity, marry one another in order to bring the male and female sides together in order to "become one flesh." But eunuchs were thought of as being closer to having both sides in balance within themselves.[6] This is why eunuchs were often referred to as "the holy ones" in ancient times and were elevated to serve in (non-Jewish) temples and royal courts. They were often placed in positions of highest trust and responsibility and often rose to senior government roles.

In Acts chapter eight, we find the story of an Ethiopian eunuch who was the Treasurer to the Queen of Ethiopia (Acts 8:27). Just like gay, lesbian, and bisexual people today, eunuchs were the sexual outcasts of Jewish religious society. The first-century teachers of Jewish law forbade converting such a person to Judaism, and they would have informed the Ethiopian eunuch when he arrived in Jerusalem that he could not even enter the outer court of the temple.

The Bible says that when Philip met the Ethiopian eunuch, he was reading from the Book of Isaiah. Perhaps someone had told him about Isaiah 56:3-5, which promises eunuchs who keep God's Word that someday they will receive a house, a monument, and a name within God's walls. The Bible says he was returning from Jerusalem when Peter met him. He may have felt discouraged because the

Jewish people were still practicing the command in Deuteronomy 23:1, which forbade him from "entering the assembly of God's people." Perhaps, like many LGBTQ Christians today, he had gone to his religious leaders with this text from Isaiah, which affirmed him, hoping he might be accepted. On his journey back home, he's reading through this scroll of Isaiah about another one of God's children who had been despised, rejected, and cut off.

The Bible says that Philip was guided by the Holy Spirit and asked the eunuch, "Do you understand what you are reading?" The Ethiopian eunuch responded: "How can I unless someone guides me?" (Acts 8:31). So Philip started with the Scripture he was reading in Isaiah and "proclaimed to him the good news of Jesus" (Acts 8:35). Then, when they came to some water, the eunuch asked Philip, "What is to prevent me from being baptized?" Philip's answer should be astonishing to anyone who still holds prejudice against LGBTQ people.

Philip responded: "If you believe with all your heart, you may." Philip didn't use Deuteronomy 23:1 as a deterrent from allowing this eunuch to come to faith in Jesus. His belief was all that was necessary.

To this day, Ethiopia has a strong Christian presence, and they credit their spiritual ancestry back to Ethiopia's first missionary — a eunuch. A man, whom the culture of the time would have regarded as one of a class of people commonly associated with homosexuality, was the first to bring the gospel to the nation of Ethiopia.

Summary of the Bible's Teaching on Homosexuality

So what have we learned about the only six passages in the Bible that seem to speak negatively towards homosexual behavior?

Sodom and Gomorrah address gang rape, not a loving relationship. The destruction of Sodom and Gomorrah is commonly assumed to have resulted from God's wrath against homosexuality. Still, the only form of same-sex behavior described in the story is an attempted gang rape (Genesis 19:5)—nothing like the loving, committed relationships that are widespread today. The Bible explicitly condemns Sodom for its arrogance, inhospitality, and apathy toward the poor, but never same-sex behavior.

The prohibitions in Leviticus don't apply to Christians. Leviticus condemns male same-sex intercourse (Leviticus 18:22 and 20:13). Still, the entire Old Testament law code has never applied to Christians in light of Christ's death. Moreover, the prohibitions of male same-sex relations reflect culturally-bound concerns about patriarchal gender roles, which the New Testament points us beyond. Not only that, but the language being used (*ish* vs. *zachar*) indicate that this may have also referred to pederasty.

Romans 1 addresses unrestrained lust, not sexual orientation. In the ancient world, it was assumed that all people could be satisfied with heterosexual sex, but some people went beyond it due to their insatiable lust—leading them to engage in same-sex behavior. Paul isn't condemning being gay as opposed to being straight. Instead, he is condemning self-seeking excess as opposed to moderation—a concern made clear by his repeated use of the term "lustful," and by his description of people "exchanging" or "abandoning" heterosexual sex.

1 Corinthians and 1 Timothy address exploitation. The Greek words used by Paul in 1 Corinthians 6:9 and 1 Timothy 1:10 (*malakoi* and *arsenokoitai*) may have referred to certain forms of same-sex behavior, but most likely exploitative forms. In order to be faithful to Scripture, we must recognize a distinction between the same-sex

behavior the Bible condemns and the desires of LGBTQ Christians for love, companionship, and family today.

Marriage is about covenant. According to Ephesians, marriage is fundamentally about commitment—keeping our covenant with our spouse as a reflection of God's own covenant with us through Jesus. The Bible doesn't teach that marriage requires procreation or gender hierarchy. Instead, it teaches that the essence of marriage is covenantal love and faithfulness, and Christian same-sex couples live out that vision of marriage every day.[7]

Being gay and Christian isn't a contradiction. The idea that the Bible is against homosexuality is a misconception that comes from people's lack of knowledge about the culture, context, and language of the Bible and a misunderstanding as to how the Bible should be read and understood today. My theological belief is that all loving relationships are honored by God. Therefore, I do not believe that the Bible speaks against loving, committed homosexual relationships.

While the six passages that address same-sex eroticism in the ancient world are negative about the practices they mention, there is no evidence that these in any way speak to same-sex relationships of love and mutuality. On the contrary, every single passage involves sexual exploitation, temple prostitution, and idolatry. There were dozens of words for gay relationships in both the Hebrew and Greek languages, and those words are not used in the Hebrew Bible or the New Testament. Instead, the clear context is about people who were offering their bodies or the bodies of others as sexual sacrifices to appease these gods and goddesses. That is what is being condemned. In that practice, men would have sex with men and women with women — but that's not the same as a same-sex relationship.

To the "Christians" that say that unrepentant homosexuals are going to hell… nothing could be further from the truth. The Scriptures say that God is fundamentally love, and perfect love casts out all fear because fear has to do with judgment. Any theology that stokes fear and any theology that's rooted in judgment is not of God. It is a false gospel. It is not good news.

I cannot believe for a moment that God would say to someone, "I am punishing you and sending you to hell because you are black." Or "I will punish you because you are a woman. You should've been a man." Neither can I understand a God who would say, "I punish you because you are homosexual. You should've been heterosexual." I can't for the life of me believe that's how God sees things.

The Good News of Jesus is this: no matter who you are, God's love will cover you in the end. No matter what you've done, God's grace is extended to you. No matter what circumstances you find yourself in life, God is with you and will never leave you nor forsake you. Being a Christian means that you follow the example of Jesus, and you receive God's grace when you do fail.

Questions to ask your gay loved one

The church has done a great deal of talking about us but rarely has spoken with us. So what is there to fear? Why the exclusion? Why the lack of conversation? It's essential to remind churches that having conversations about us, without us, is nothing more than a recycling of preconceived ideas, misconceptions, and talking points.
Here are some great questions to ask and have a conversation with your gay loved one:

- "What was it like to sit in church and hear the word 'abomination' used to describe you?"

- "What was it like to get to the point of accepting that you were gay and coming out, knowing you might be rejected by those you love and the church and God you've served?"
- "How did you find resolution of your Christian beliefs and your sexuality?"
- "When you came out to your Christian friends at church and they told you that you could never fall in love or have a partner of life as they could — how did that make you feel?"
- "What did if feel like when your megachurch pastor said you couldn't serve coffee to people after church because you'd shared with him you were in a committed, monogamous three-year relationship?"
- "How did you feel when you confided in your pastor that you thought you might be gay, resulting in him removing you from the kids ministry you loved so much, even though you had never acted on those feelings?"

Shame dies when stories are told in safe places. In listening to our stories, you will learn. Once people realize how normal we are and see themselves in us, homophobia and controversy will be over. A mark of an open mind is being more committed to your curiosity than to your convictions. The goal of learning is not to shield old views against new facts. It's to revise old views to incorporate new facts. Ideas are possibilities to explore, not certainties to defend.

Remember Brene Brown's definition of shame from an earlier chapter? It's the fear of disconnection. So how do we help our loved ones heal from shame? First, remember that shame is a social construct. It happens between people. Therefore the best way to heal from shame is through people.

Receiving empathy from those whom you love the most is the number one way to help your gay loved one heal from their shame. And hopefully, you're no longer in the "love the sinner but hate the sin" category after reading this book and examining the evidence for yourself.

Your gay or lesbian loved one will experience empathy when you show them with your words, eyes, or actions that you actually do "get" how it feels to be one of us. It's the most essential healing experience your loved one can have outside of intense therapy.

Coming out to the people we care about is perhaps the most crucial aspect in healing that shame. Holding secrets can be absolutely traumatizing. There's even research to prove this. People who experience rape or sexual abuse sometimes find that hiding the traumatic event and not discussing it with others can be more traumatic than the actual event itself. Psychologists today tell us that trauma is what happens to us when there is an absence of an empathetic witness.

As your gay loved one takes baby steps towards being open and vulnerable with you — please be "safe enough" in your reaction and response so that they don't regret this decision and fall into more mental, emotional, and spiritual damage.

Loving Reminders for Those Who Are Gay

L.R. Knost wrote these words that should be a great reminder to those of us within the LGBTQ community: "Do not be dismayed by the brokenness of the world. All things break. And all things can be mended. Not with time, as they say but with intention. So go. Love intentionally, extravagantly, unconditionally. The broken world waits in darkness for the light that is you."

For my gay brothers and sisters reading this book, I want to remind you that it serves no one for us to live less than we are. That means no more hiding or pretending you are straight. Stop being afraid. Stop being ashamed and wondering what others will think of you if they knew. Have the courage to face your fears and not allow other people to think less of you. Don't let anyone get comfortable disrespecting you. Never let another soul on this earth make you feel like you're not enough. An entire sea of water can't sink a ship unless it gets inside the ship.

Similarly, the world's negativity can't put you down unless you allow it to get inside of you. The time comes when we must resist always meeting the expectations of others and ask them to meet us where we are. Your coming out journey is a liberation from a host of unclean spirits and destructive forces that have deceived you into believing evil things and rejecting yourself and your own reality.

In 2000, Tammy Baldwin, a lesbian and member of the United States House of Representatives, from the district of Wisconsin, spoke from the stage of the Millennium March on Washington: "If you dream of a world in which you can put your partner's picture on your desk, then put his picture on your desk and you will live in such a world." In her inspiring speech to hundreds of thousands attending, she continued on to say, "Remember, there are two things that keep us oppressed: them and us. We are half of the equation. There will not be a magic day when we wake up and it's now OK to express ourselves publicly. We must make that day ourselves, by speaking out publicly — first in small numbers, then in greater numbers, until its simply the way things are and no one thinks twice." [8]

We are half of the equation. We can create this day by being true to ourselves. When we choose to be our most authentic and loving selves, we leave a trail of magic everywhere we go. As Shauna

Niequist so aptly worded: "What kills a soul? Exhaustion, secret-keeping, image management. And what brings a soul back from the dead? Honesty, connection, grace." You can't win the war against the world if you can't win the battle against your own mind.

One day a man was crossing a bridge in life but was scared, so he turned and asked God, "Can I hold your hand so I may not fall?"

God said, "No, my child, I will hold your hand."

The man asked, "What's the difference?"

God replied, "If you hold my hand and something happens, you might let go, but if I hold your hand, no matter what happens, I will never let go of you."

If today you feel like God has abandoned you as an LGBTQ person, I hope that you will come to realize that our God "will never leave you nor forsake you." He is still there with you…holding your hand tightly. He will never let you go.

WHERE I AM TODAY

"Embrace uncertainty. Some of the most beautiful chapters in our lives won't have a title until much later."

– Bob Goff

As I look back over the last three years, it sometimes feels surreal to think about how much my life has changed. Many aspects of life have drastically improved; some things have become more challenging. Such is the balance of life.

"What are you doing these days?" is the question I often get asked from folks who knew me when I was a pastor. I've honestly been living a tranquil and peaceful life. Ministry has a way of causing you to always be in the public eye. You live in the proverbial glass house. Yet now, I had seemingly gone "off the radar." So moving across state lines to Kansas to live in a quiet condo overlooking a peaceful creek and golf course has been a welcome respite for a soul that was always on full display.

In a way, my calling hasn't changed; it has only shifted. My life purpose statement I wrote many years ago was, "To become the best version of myself and help others do the same." That purpose has never changed. I'm no longer the megachurch pastor speaking to thousands across multiple campuses; I'm just influencing people from the sidelines. I'm now self-employed, running my own business — *Park Enterprises.* I'm in the personal growth and development industry seeking to inspire others through resources, online courses, coaching, content-creation, book writing, and motivational speaking. Coaching others in both an individual and group setting and helping them navigate the challenges they face and reach their personal goals brings me so much joy each day. Speaking has always been my first career love. And I'm slowly allowing myself to reclaim the stage in corporate events as well as within New Thought and gay-affirming churches. The words of Ram Dass ring true to me: "The more conscious a being becomes, the more he can use any occupation as a vehicle for spreading light."

Besides my immediate family, I really don't have much connection to the people who used to know me before my divorce and "being outed." So many people from my past know a version of me that, quite frankly, doesn't exist anymore. I've grown so much in my understanding and self-awareness that I sometimes feel unrecognizable to myself, let alone others. Whenever I do interact with people from my "former life," — I feel the pressure to put the "Pastor Mask" back on and try to resume acting the role of the person they remember me as. Now that I've healed from so much, it's repulsive to me to attempt to project an image inauthentic to who I am at my core.

A part of me feels guilty when I've declined invitations to reconnect with those of my former life for coffee or lunch. Nevertheless, the person they once knew no longer exists. How do I encapsulate in one meeting over coffee the immense growth journey and the depth of understanding that has led me to where I am today?

Not only that, but I've discerned that some have ulterior motives for wanting to meet with me. It's not because they care. It's because they want information. As a pastor to thousands, everyone once had access to me. Today, this is not the case. Not everyone has access to me because I want peace more than attention. For far too long, the expectations of others were the bars I used to build my own cage. I have now set myself free. Life is simpler when you stop explaining yourself to people and just do what works for you.

> The expectations of others were the bars I used to build my own cage. I have now set myself free. Life is simpler when you stop explaining yourself to people and just do what works for you.

Healing from Divorce

Our marriage came to an official conclusion on Valentine's Day of 2020 when the judge signed the divorce papers. It was also the same day we closed on selling the home that our family had shared together. I met my now ex-wife at the title company and brought her a cup of coffee. We both felt relief that this long journey was finally over, and now we were splitting the equity in our home and collecting our respective checks.

I had always given my wife a gift on Valentine's Day, and I felt that it was fitting that I should give her one last parting gift. In the year leading up to our divorce, I kept a gratitude journal where I would write down one thing I appreciated about her or felt gratitude towards her on that day. I wish I could say that I had made a journal entry all 365 days, but I did manage to make about 180 if I remember correctly. I'm so glad God led me to do that. You always see what you are looking for when it comes to your relationships. It seems strange to say this, but my last year of marriage to my wife was my favorite year in many ways. Partly because I was more conscious in looking for the good in who she was and how she enhanced the lives of my three kids and me. With the sudden turn of events in our marriage and subsequent divorce, I never had the opportunity to give her this journal I had been working so long to create. But I now knew that I needed to give it. I wanted her to know and be reminded of what an incredible woman she truly is. She didn't ask for any of this. She didn't sign up to be in a mixed-orientation marriage. She didn't deserve to be married to someone who was unable to love himself, therefore unable to fully give her the love and type of relationship that she deserved.

I had also taken that same little teddy bear — the "I Love You Bear" that we had traded back and forth all throughout our years of marriage together. I would be giving it to her one last time. So, along with the gratitude journal I made for her, I tucked this little stuffed animal inside the gift bag, along with my wedding ring sewed onto the heart held by the teddy bear. It was my last and final way of expressing to her, "I love you."

I couldn't stand to watch her open the gift. I turned away and got into my car and sobbed all the way home. I had to pull the car over at one point because I could no longer see the road through my tears. Memories from the last 15 years flooded my mind as tears flowed down my face. She was the only person I had ever loved. Yet now, the journey of our lives was taking us in new and separate directions. In a way, I feel like I will always love her because she will forever be a part of my life — not just because she's the mother of our beautiful children, and we will raise our grandchildren together. But because of the many beautiful memories we shared along the way during our many years together.

Even though the divorce was brutally painful, I've grown to love and appreciate her in new ways as the co-parent of our children. She's even adopted my new puppy Milo as her own, and he loves to go to her house to play. The bitterness and anger that often comes with divorce gave way to love, grace, and peace as I could now view her from afar and see her as a beautiful soul in the image of God. In a strange sort of way, I feel like we lived up to our marriage vows, at least partially. I think we both knew that the only way we could keep that vow of honoring one another was to let each other go. Sometimes divorce is not about renouncing your vows as much as it is releasing your vows. When we think of a relationship that was "meant to be," we automatically assume it's forever. But maybe it's not supposed to last forever. Maybe people come and go in our lives to teach us something. Maybe the "forever" is not the person, but what we gain and learn from them along the journey of our shared experience together.

I wanted our "conscious uncoupling" to be an example to others that you can still remain wonderful friends with your ex-spouse. I'm so grateful that I had those 15 years of incredible memories with her. Christmas came during the time when we were in the middle of our divorce proceedings. We decided to spend Christmas together with the kids and exchange gifts just as we had always done. That year I gave her a piece of jewelry with the Scripture of Psalm 46:5 engraved on it: *"God is within her, she will not fail."* That was my daily prayer for the woman who was becoming my ex-wife. I had always enjoyed being the provider for her and the kids, but now she would be on her own, and I was praying and believing that she would more than thrive beyond anything I could imagine. God has answered and continues to answer that prayer. Today, she seems happy and flourishing as a real estate agent, and she has since gotten remarried to a wonderful man. I couldn't be any happier for the both of them. They are both such a blessing to me to this day.

Alone, But Not Lonely

Unless my kids are here, I live alone. Yet, for the most part, I'm so content and happy. I can honestly say I've enjoyed this new season of singlehood. So much so, that I sometimes wonder if I could ever live under the same roof with someone again. Of course, I have a desire to share my life with a soulmate, but I'm perfectly content to wait until the right one comes along.

There's a vast difference between being lonely and being alone. I've found it to be so healthy for me to spend time alone. A season of loneliness and isolation is when the caterpillar gets its wings. It seems like the older I get, the more I appreciate having time just with myself.

> A season of loneliness and isolation is when the caterpillar gets its wings.

Every person who is single needs to be alone, at least for a season, to not be defined by another person. Until you get comfortable with being by yourself, you'll never know if you're choosing another person out of love or out of loneliness. One of the biggest mistakes single people make after ending a relationship is immediately starting a new one. We immediately rush into another relationship, thinking it will make everything better... but it rarely does. The space after a relationship is to find yourself... not someone else. As Rumi once said, "If you are never alone, you cannot know yourself. And if you do not know yourself, you will begin to fear the void." The reward of loneliness is the knowledge of ourselves.

I've tried to heed the words of Diana Sparacino, who wrote:

> Be alone. Eat alone. Take yourself on dates. Sleep alone. In the midst of this, you will learn about yourself. You will grow, you will figure out what inspires you, you will curate your own dreams, your own beliefs, your own stunning clarity, and when you do meet the person who makes your cells dance, you will be sure of it, because you are sure of yourself.

What you discover about yourself without the distractions of others being present is mind-blowing. Eckhart Tolle said, "You find peace not by rearranging the circumstances of your life, but by realizing who you are at the deepest level."

Cultivating Authenticity

Today, I no longer feel as though I'm living someone else's life. The separation between who I was on the inside and what I do on the outside no longer suffocates my soul. The idea of integrity in the strictest sense means being whole and complete — where your internal convictions and external actions are in alignment. To live a life of integrity is to live with wholeness where all aspects of your life integrate. Nothing is splintered off or compartmentalized. Instead, everything fits and aligns together into one homogenous whole. And once you unify sexuality with your spirituality and religiosity, you become an unstoppable power.

> Today, I no longer feel as though I'm living someone else's life.

There's a children's book written in 1922 that I really resonate within this stage of my life. *The Velveteen Rabbit* is a story about a stuffed animal's desire to become real through the love of his owner. In many ways, I find it symbolic of my journey towards authenticity through the love of my Owner, God Himself. Here's an excerpt from this book:

> He said, "You become. It takes a long time. That's why it doesn't happen often to people who break easily, or have sharp edges, or who have to be carefully kept. Generally, by the time you are Real, most of you hair has been loved off, and your eyes drop out and you get loose in the joints and very shabby. But these things don't matter at all, because once you are Real you can't be ugly, except to people who don't understand."

Lessons Learned

Over the last three years, I have gone through the process of unlearning everything I believed about myself. I had to unlearn much in order to discover the truth. And these are some of the life lessons I've found along the way:[1]

- I wasn't sick or in need of healing — there was already a wholeness in me that I needed to believe and live by.
- I wasn't broken or in need of fixing — I was already whole and complete.
- There's great freedom that comes from being so confident in who you are that no one's opinion, rejection, or behavior can rock you. The version of me that others create in their minds is not my responsibility.
- I was worthy of being fully known and fully loved. I no longer needed to hide parts of me in shame. I am perfectly imperfect.
- I wasn't an abomination to God — I am loved by him and an equal to every other human being that walks on this planet, entitled to the respect and rights that brings with it.
- I'm no longer living with the core beliefs of feeling unlovable, unworthy, or not enough. I am love. I'm worthy of love. And I am enough…just the way I am.
- It wasn't my homosexuality that was keeping me in bondage — but my own ignorance and the ignorance of my culture around sexual orientation.
- True self-love and self-acceptance are absolutely liberating — shame and self-loathing are the most destructive forces in the human psyche.
- To define homosexuality in terms of an act or behavior is limited — my sexual orientation is so much more. It's about a sense of self, identity, love, intimacy, affection, and partnering with someone of the same gender as opposed to the opposite.

- As a gay man, I am not destined to live a life of loneliness — I don't need someone else or to be in a relationship for me to be happy. I find so much joy and contentment in my relationship with God and the newfound sincere and genuine friends that treat me like family. I have so much love in my heart to give to others, and I don't necessarily need a relationship to do so.
- Saying that you know the "truth" makes everyone who thinks differently than you wrong. It puts you in the dangerous position of never being open to learning and discovering anything new.
- In life's journey, you are never off the path. Every detour, dead-end, back alley, and even complete road wrecks are all a part of this marvelous journey when viewed with deep insight.

Today, I live with absolutely no regrets. In life, we do things. Some we wish we had never done. Some we wish we could replay a million times differently in our heads. But they all make us who we are, and in the end, they shape every detail about us. To love who you are, you cannot hate the experiences that shaped you. Even though what I've gone through has been difficult, and the heart-wrenching emotions of it all nearly brought me to the end of life itself — I look back on my journey now with a great sense of gratitude. Had I not been born with this sexual orientation, there are lessons about myself and that nature of reality that I would not have learned any other way. New beginnings are often disguised as painful endings.

> To love who you are, you cannot hate the experiences that shaped you.

Releasing the Hurt

I've learned to let go and release any hard feelings or unforgiveness I've harbored in my heart towards others. Bitterness has been defined as ingesting the poison you intended for another. Forgiveness is setting the prisoner free only to realize you were the prisoner. I had decided to forgive friends that had betrayed me and those who had let me down. Only after letting all of that go would I be free to move on.

It's interesting how in life, not a single scar on our hearts comes from an enemy. I am learning that people come into your life for a reason, a season, or for treason — the trick is to determine who is there for what purpose. Just as Jesus couldn't get to the cross without Judas, even the people who betray you are all part of the ultimate plan.

The mind replays what the heart can't delete. Forgiveness and letting go is the only way to find peace and be free — you can't reach for anything new if your hands are still full of yesterday's junk. There's a Chinese proverb that says, "He who blames others has a long way to go on his journey. He who blames himself is halfway there. He who blames no one has arrived."

Most people never heal because they stay in their heads, replaying corrupted scenarios. I knew I must let it all go. Everything in life is a result of your story. You're either re-telling the story of your past or creating a new story of your future. I'm choosing to no longer re-read old chapters. I'm writing new ones.

Experiencing Deep Healing

Healing had come to me in areas I never thought possible. My life had fallen apart, but it had also fallen together at the same time. The many who had walked out of my life have been replaced by the many who have walked in. Every loss has led to a greater gain. Every situation that hasn't worked out has led me to a greater one. Every bad chapter has taught me deeper wisdom. If I can trust a puzzle company to make sure every piece is in the box to complete the puzzle, I know I can trust my Creator that every piece of my life is there for a reason. So now, when things go left, I know it's for something else to go right. I love who I've been, but now I really love who I'm becoming.

I'm not saying that I don't have bad days, that I don't still cry, that I don't still feel the aftershocks of shame, or that I no longer struggle with loneliness. But I will tell you this: the gap between who I am and who I want to be is a lot smaller than it used to be.

> One of the happiest moments in your life is when you find the courage to accept what you can't change.

One of the happiest moments in your life is when you find the courage to accept what you can't change. You cannot control what comes next. Living in the present without attaching your happiness to any future outcome is what brings you peace. When you live in the complete acceptance of what is, that is the absolute end of all drama in your life.

When you're in a dark place, you sometimes think you've been buried. Perhaps you've been planted. Just as a seed must be broken to dig its roots, so your life and mine must be broken before it can bloom.

Today I don't suffer from any internal suffering or shame. There are days when I do feel it externally, though. As a gay Christian man, you're always perceptive and sometimes hyper-sensitive to how society thinks and responds to you. For the most part, I am entirely comfortable with my sexuality. I am not an activist, but I am comfortable to the point where I no longer fear people's reaction to me being gay. For me, this journey of coming to grips with the conclusions I've shared in this book has been liberating. With my own questions answered and my own personal issues resolved, there is nothing anyone could do or say that could shake the belief that now resides in myself and my relationship with God. The overwhelming sense of peace and freedom is incredible. I will never again allow myself to internalize another person's judgment or condemnation of me. No one has that kind of power over my life.

Finding a New Community

My compassion for others and my empathy towards those who are different has expanded tremendously. The love and welcome reception that I've been given by the gay community has been overwhelmingly at times. So much so that I've often wondered: "Where was this type of love, acceptance, and camaraderie within the church?" I never knew it was possible to truly be loved and valued just for being you — bringing nothing else to the table.

When I was a pastor, I never really knew who my real friends were. You quickly discover that those whom you think are your friends are really only close to you for strategic or political purposes. They are your "friend" because of what they stand to gain from being in close proximity to you. Yet once I was no longer a pastor with influence, they had no use for me. They didn't bother to return my calls. And once my life fell apart, I felt utterly deserted by them.

It's hard to judge others when you feel like you're still on trial yourself.

Yet now, I've been introduced to a community that is so openly accepting and authentic. They are some of the most open-minded people you'll ever meet, perhaps because it's hard to judge others when you feel like you're still on trial yourself. They quickly move to reach out to the outsiders because they don't want others to feel the pain they have had to experience in their life. The reason why gay people are so kind is because the world has been so unkind to them. They don't want others to encounter hurt and unacceptance the way they did. Sometimes the strongest people are not those who show strength in front of us but those who win battles we know nothing about. That is certainly true for most gay men and women I've had the privilege to get to know.

Navigating Dating

Now that I live as a single, somewhat-freshly-divorced-40-year-old, I sometimes wonder if I'll ever find that soulmate. Would there be anyone I could build dreams with, grow old with, and hold my hand when I die?

Sure, I have plenty of guys eager to date me, which certainly makes me feel wanted and validated. But the reality is, my life experience has brought me through so much. I've grown so drastically as a result that it's hard to find someone with enough emotional intelligence and self-awareness who thinks and lives on the same level. I don't say that arrogantly, but the reality is that most people have never done the deeper work that's necessary to live authentically and purposefully. People can only meet you as deeply as they've met themselves. People can only love to their level of self-love; communicate to their level of self-awareness; and behave to their level of healed trauma. So my goal has been to work on becoming the best version of myself, believing that by doing so, I will attract others who are also blooming into my life. What attracts me most are individuals who are growing and expanding to reach their fullest potential. Just by being around them —they're helping me become the best version of myself as well. I've spent my lifetime pouring into others, and I hope to find a life partner who can mutually pour back into me. I feel most fulfilled in relationships where I'm constantly learning from them as they're pursue their own unique journey of spiritual and personal growth. As a result, our vibes resonate together in harmony as we discover that we're so much better together than we are apart.

Still, those nagging questions persist: "What would happen if I never find anyone?" I've often thought. "Would that mean that I would spend the rest of my life being unhappy?" I've resolved that I can live a very fulfilled and rewarding life as a single man and not wait for someone else to make me happy. So I'm not searching or waiting for anyone. For the first time, I'm enjoying my life to it's fullest.

I appreciate the teachings found in the book *The Five Love Languages*, meaning that we give and receive love in five primary ways: words of affirmation, gifts, physical touch, acts of service, and quality time. We all desire to show that love towards someone else, but has it ever occurred to you that you can give and receive those expressions of love to yourself? I take myself out on dates to dinner and a movie. I buy myself gifts (no one buys me better gifts than the ones I buy for myself). I sometimes recite a list of positive affirmations to myself in the mirror. I spend quality time alone in nature, journaling and asking myself probing questions to become more aware of the essence that is "me."

> The love you deserve is already within you. Start giving it to yourself. You don't need someone else to be loved... you are love.

The love you deserve is already within you. Start giving it to yourself. You don't need someone else to be loved... you are love. Don't believe me? How do you have so much love to give to others? You can't pour water out of an empty cup. That's why Jesus said we should "love our neighbor...as we love ourselves." The more time I spend loving myself, the more I find this overwhelming desire to pour our more live into the lives of those around me.

The Gift of Being an Outsider

I've come to see that being ostracized and alienated from the institutionalized Church I had once devoted my life to is actually a precious gift. A gift I would never have known living behind the facade of those church walls. There were too many things standing in the way between me and the truth: constraints, expectations, perceptions, dogma, and doctrine. All of which seemed important and real at the time but now I view much of them as actual barriers to true discovery and freedom.

Although I still feel like an outsider from the evangelical church, I have found a growing number of affirming churches that not only welcome me but even desire me to speak. I believe that the tide is slowly shifting. I may perhaps always feel ostracized from the faith community I was raised in. Some find it difficult to reconcile the fact that I, like a growing number around the world, could be gay and yet still be able to find peace and resolution with my faith and have a thriving relationship with God. Others avoid me, choosing to think of me as an apostate that should be shunned. I hold no grudges. I've been where they are. Everyone is doing the very best they can to live and make sense of this world according to their current level of consciousness. It's ok that those bridges have been burnt. Sometimes you get the best light from a burning bridge. A light that shows you a new path forward to a new future.

> Everyone is doing the very best they can to live and make sense of this world according to their current level of consciousness.

Albert Einstein said, "The one who follows the crowd will usually go no further than the crowd. The one who walks alone is likely to find himself in places no one has ever been before." I certainly feel that that is true for me.

Forging a New Spiritual Path

My journey has taken on a whole new path of discovery and self-awareness. I'm now living life on a totally different level, with such a profound level of fulfillment.

What I've noticed with others who have gone through similar experiences as me is that reaching your breaking point many times leads you down a path towards spirituality. That certainly is true of me as I began my spiritual awakening journey in 2019. Religion is for people who fear hell; spirituality is for people who have been there. I am a follower of Jesus, and yet I'd consider myself now more spiritual than religious. I'm learning that we're already in the presence of God. What's absent is awareness. I'm learning to just walk in daily surrender to the Divine, and just show up in response to what God brings to my day.

Strangely, my relationship with God today feels more intimate than it's ever been before. Which admitted feels odd for someone who used to "speak on behalf of God" as a pastor. Maybe it's this new awareness. Maybe it's because God and I have been together through some really tough shit. Maybe it's how I've come to experience God through extended times of meditation. All I know is that things are different...and I love this state of being so much more. I don't believe in God... I *know* God. I've found that even belief in the Divine is only a poor substitute for the living reality of God manifesting every moment of your life. My new favorite word to understand and describe God is "Source." From my relationship with that divine energy, I receive all that I have, and walk in the awareness of all that I am. Every morning when I wake up, I whisper a quiet two-word prayer: "Thank you." I was once a man on the verge of ending it all not too long ago, but now I'm so appreciative of this ravishing gift called "Life." My love and gratitude for God as my Source grows exponentially with each passing day.

I began to set intentions and see God answer prayers in unmistakable and miraculous ways. I even started keeping a log of all of these answered prayers. Who knows... maybe someday I'll turn that log into another book. I've found that God seems to be answering my prayers more now, as a man who has accepted his sexuality — than I ever did as a pastor. Which, admittedly, still seems ironic to me. I used to teach that it wasn't supposed to work that way.

> God is so much bigger and so much more unfathomable, mysterious, and marvelous than the tiny box that many evangelical Christians have put Him in.

My spiritual awakening has taught me more about God in three years than what I thought I knew about Him during my two decades in full-time ministry. God is so much bigger and so much more unfathomable, mysterious, and marvelous than the tiny box that many evangelical Christians have put Him in.

The most astounding experiences of synchronicity (or "divine appointments," if you will) occur almost daily as I frequently find myself in the right place at the right time to meet the right individuals. It's as if finding healing in myself and rediscovering my life purpose drew the right people and circumstances towards me effortlessly like a magnet. Those who walk with healing become agents of healing.

The people that I find myself called to serve and to build my new tribe with are those individuals who are not necessarily "religious" but have a deep sense of spirituality and a desire to know God. Many of them have been hurt, disappointed, and/or disenfranchised by the Church. I would have never been in a position to have an influence on these beautiful people if I were still hiding behind those stained-glass windows. I have come to the remarkable discovery that my own alienation from the church was a precious gift. My homosexuality set the stage for me to become an outcast. But I now believe that that has pointed me towards my ultimate purpose, which is to help everyone who feels like a castaway to know that God has a seat at the table just for them. I was made an outsider to reach the outsiders.

The calling on my life is just as strong today as when I was ordained into the ministry at the age of 18. I've had several of my new friends ask me to consider starting a church — a different kind of church — to reach those who are disenfranchised or ostracized from traditional church. After pastoring churches for nearly two decades, the thought of going back to that doesn't appeal to me. The words "church" and "pastor" inherit a certain set of expectations that I am willing to leave behind and not pick up again. I do, however, want to help create an environment where hungry people can meet God and grow together -- "to become the best version of themselves and help others do the same."

So what's the next step for me? As I'm now on my 40th lap around the sun, this year is the year I'm starting a new venture that I feel encapsulates the full spectrum of who I am and what I've done. I started a new organization called *The Apex Collective*. The word "apex" simply means "the top or highest point of something." My goal is to facilitate an environment for a collective group of individuals — who all desire to reach their highest potential, to expand their consciousness, and to know God's purpose for their lives. As a non-profit, we will function as a center for spirituality and personal growth — that literally anyone and everyone is welcome to be a part of, regardless of their walk in life. The goal is for all of us to learn and grow from one another's collective knowledge and experience. I'll facilitate the teaching of lessons on different personal development topics, complete with notes to accelerate learning, and then allow others to ask questions or share what they know about the subject as well. As a collective, we'll be equipped to coach others towards reaching the apex of their life experience, and we'll strategize ways for us to bring help, healing, and wholeness to our community. I'm excited to grow our tribe!

Moving Forward

Just as grapes must be crushed to make wine, diamonds form under pressure, and seeds grow in darkness — it was within the place of utter destitution where God met me. Whenever you feel crushed, under pressure, or in darkness, just remember... you too are in a powerful place of transformation.

Sometimes life gives you the gift of standing outside of yourself, if only for a moment — in order to help you see where you've been and where you're going; how your current understanding differs from what you used to believe.

It's a strange paradox. Whenever I focused on becoming a "good Christian," I felt like it was making me a bad human. But when I strived towards becoming a good human being, I found that it made me a better Christian.

I made a career out of teaching the Bible. One of the reasons I went into full-time ministry was because I wanted to know Jesus better by studying the Bible. What I have discovered in the years since I've resigned as a pastor is that Jesus gives a very different picture of God than the fundamentalist church currently sometimes does.

Where the church demands, "Be holy!" Jesus whispers, "Be with me."

Where the church says, "Call out the sinner!" Jesus says, "Reach out to the broken."

Where the church says, "Where the church warns, "The path is narrow and few find it." Jesus, the Shepherd, says, "Out of my one hundred sheep, I'll leave the ninety-nine to find the lost one."

Where the church cries, "Vengeance belongs to God!" Jesus weeps, "Father, forgive them!"

Where the church claims, "God's justice is not diminished by his love." Jesus says, "Divine love demands a justice that means victory for all, and all means all." [2]

In many ways, it's a matter of what we focus on: the old or the new; the letter or the spirit; partial revelation or full revelation. Regardless, Scripture teaches us that we all "see through a glass, darkly" (1 Corinthians 13:12), and if that's the case, our love, grace, understanding, and empathy of others should be overwhelmingly abundant.

So where do I go from here as a recovering pastor and as a gay Christian? I'll trust the next chapter of my life because I know the Author. Wherever my path unfolds, I think I'll stick with the one I began this journey with in the first place many years ago as a child...

I'll stick with Jesus.

"I Love You"

Means

That I accept you for the person that you are, and that I do not wish to change you into someone else. It means that I will love you and stand by you even through the worst of times. It means loving you even when you're in a bad mood, or too tired to do the things I want to do. It means loving you when you're down, not just when you're fun to be with. "I love you" means that I know your deepest secrets and do not judge you for them, asking in return that you do not judge me for mine. It means that I care enough to fight for what we have and that I love you enough not to let go. It means thinking of you, dreaming of you, and hoping you feel the same way about me.

"You must love in such a way that the person
you love feels free."
- Thich Nhat Hanh

NOTES

Walk a Mile in My Shoes

[1] I owe much of the credit to the content of this chapter from the writings of Alan Downs in his book Velvet Rage: Overcoming the Pain of Growing up Gay in a Straight Man's World. I highly recommend everyone interested in this topic to buy this book.

[2] "Is Homosexuality a Choice?" Scientific American. https://blogs.scientificamerican.com/guest-blog/is-homosexuality-a-choice/

The Choice No On Chooses

[1] Adapted from the research found in the documentary, *For the Bible Tells Me So*.

[2] "Is Homosexuality a Choice?" Scientific American. https://blogs.scientificamerican.com/guest-blog/is-homosexuality-a-choice/

[3] Ibid.

[4] "The Verdict Is In: Homosexuality is Not a Choice," Health 24 News. https://www.news24.com/health24/sex/sexual-diversity/the-verdict-is-in-homosexuality-is-not-a-choice-20150807

[5] See the YouTube video from the Today Show, "Same-Sex Penguin Couple 'Adopts' Abandoned Egg at Zoo" at https://www.youtube.com/watch?v=Cgj7Wg1_Yc4

Genesis 19 – The Untold Story of Sodom

[1] Adam Hamilton, *Making Sense of the Bible*, pg. 268

Leviticus 18 & 20 – The Abominations

[1] Dr. David Ben-Gad HaCohen, "Dancing Erotically with the Golden Calf." https://www.thetorah.com/article/dancing-erotically-with-the-golden-calf

[2] Corey, "For the People Who Say," para. 7.https://belover.medium.com/gays-in-the-bible-5ecf258baf0c

[3] Robert A.J. Gagnon, *The Bible and Homosexual Practice: Texts and Hermeneutics* (Nashville: Abingdon Press, 2001), 130.

Romans 1 – Rome Gone Wild!

[1] Colby Martin, UnClobber, 113.

[2] Justin Lee, Torn,

[3] Martin, Colby. UnClobber: Rethinking Our Misuse of the Bible on Homosexuality. E-book ed., Westminster John Knox Press, 2016. Kindle.

[4] Numbers 6:5 says that men who take the Nazirite vow "Must let their hair grow long" in order to set themselves apart for the Lord. 2 Samuel 14:26 praises Absalom's abundant hair, and 2 Kings 2:23 recounts how Elisha was taunted for his baldness.

[5] Vines, Matthew. God and the Gay Christian.

[6] William Sanday and Arthur C. Headlam, A Critical and Exegetical Commentary on the Epistle to the Romans, International Critical Commentary, 5th ed. (Edinburgh: T&T Clark, 1902), 50.

[7] Plutarch, Dialogue on Love, 5, quoted in Hubbard, Homosexuality, 455.

[8] Philo, On Abraham, trans. F.H. Colton (Cambridge, MA: Harvard University Press, 1954), 133-41.

[9] From the first-century Jewish text Sentences of Pseudo-Phocylides.

[10] Pseudo-Lucian, Amores; or Affairs of the Heart, quoted in Gagnon, Bible and Homosexual Practice, 166n10.

[11] Martin, Colby. UnClobber: Rethinking Our Misuse of the Bible on Homosexuality. E-book ed., Westminster John Knox Press, 2016. Kindle.

[12] Julian of Eclanum, quoted in Augustine, On Marriage and Concupiscence, bk. 2, trans. Peter Homles and Robert Enest Wallis, rev. Benjamin B. Warfield, in Nicene and Post-Nicene Fathers, 1st see., vol. 5, ed. Philip Staff (Buffalo, NY: Christians Literature Publishing, 1998).

1 Corinthians 9 & 1 Timothy 1 – Gays and the kingdom of God

[1] How to Talk About the Bible and LGBT Inclusion (The Reformation Project), 14.

[2] Shore, Unfair, 9.

[3] From the New American Bible (Revised Edition), footnote b, 1 Corinthians 6:9.

[4] John MacArthur, MacArthur New Testament Commentary, 146.

[5] See the documentary website: www.1946themovie.com for more information.

[6] Hornblower and Spawforth, Oxford Classical Dictionary, 720.

[7] Scruggs, Robin. Does the Bible NOT Oppose Homosexuality? https://www.pbs.org/wgbh/pages/frontline/shows/assault/bible/doesnotoppose.html

The Three Buckets of the Bible

[1] Hamilton, 273.

[2] Jim Lee, *Torn*, 193.

[3] Hamilton, 274. (All credit belongs to Adam Hamilton regarding the analogy of three buckets).

[4] Quote adapted from the documentary movie, *For the Bible Tells Me So.*

[5] Robert P. Vande Kappelle, *Grace Revealed: The Message of Paul's Letter to the Romans -- Then and Now.* (Wipf & Stock, 2017), 9.

[6] Dave Roos, "Who Decided Which Books to Include in the Bible?" https://people.howstuffworks.com/books-of-bible.htm

[7] Hamilton, Adam. Making Sense of the Bible. (Harper One, 2014), 133.

[8] "The Christian Case for Gay Marriage." Los Angeles Times. https://www.latimes.com/opinion/la-xpm-2012-dec-02-la-oe-pearce-christianity-gay-marriage-20121202-story.html

[9] Enns, Peter. *The Bible Tells Me So* (Harper One)

[10] https://reformationproject.org/biblical-case/

[11] Hamilton, 266.

The Love Story of David and Jonathan

[1] Jeff Miner and John Tyler Connoley, "David loved Jonathan more than women," excerpt from The Children Are Free: Reexamining the Biblical Evidence on Same-sex Relationships.

[2] Ibid.

[3] Tom Horner, Jonathan Loved David, p. 20.

Ex-Gays and Conversion Therapy

[1] Lee, Justin. Torn: Rescuing the Gospel from the Gays vs. Christians Debate (Jericho Books, 2012), 106.

[2] https://www.theguardian.com/lifeandstyle/2018/jun/10/i-was-19-gay-and-ready-to-be-cured-by-conversion-therapy

[3] https://www.theguardian.com/lifeandstyle/2018/jun/10/i-was-19-gay-and-ready-to-be-cured-by-conversion-therapy

[4] https://www.vic.gov.au/lgbtq-change-and-suppression-practices-fact-sheet

[5] Rymel, Tim. Going Gay: My Journey From Evangelical Minister to Self-Acceptance, Lovee, Life, and Meaning (CK Publishing), 189.

[6] https://www.bbc.com/news/stories-49679273

[7] Quote taken from the documentary, For They Know Not What They Do."

Marriage vs. Celibacy

[1] Slick, "What does the Bible say," para. 2

[2] Philip Pullella, "Gay Marriage a Threat to Humanity's Future: Pope," reuters.com, January 9, 2012

[3] BBC News, "Gay Marriage around the World," bbc.com, April 23, 2013

[4] Alan Cooperman, Jonathan Finer, and Fred Barbash, "Gay Couples Wed in Mass.," Washington Post, May 17, 2004

[5] New York Times, "Gay Marriage Backers Win Supreme Court Victory," nytimes.com, June 26, 2015

[6] Christy Mallory and Brad Sears, "The Economic Impact of Marriage Equality Five Years after Obergefell v. Hodges," williamsinstitute.law.ucla.edu, May 2020

[7] Harmeet Kaur, "Costa Rica Becomes the First Central American Country to Legalize Same-Sex Marriage," cnn.com, May 26, 2020

[8] Wikipedia, "Same-Sex Marriage," https://en.wikipedia.org/wiki/Same-sex_marriage#:~:text=As%20of%202021%2C%20same%2Dsex,being%20Costa%20Rica%20in%202020. March 2022.

[9] https://www.amnesty.org/en/latest/news/2018/10/its-intersex-awareness-day-here-are-5-myths-we-need-to-shatter/

[10] Poletti, Jonathan. "Did Christianity misunderstand the "Sex Rules?" https://medium.com/belover/did-christianity-misunderstand-the-sex-rules-7fd540752b9a. March 2022.

[11] Ibid.

[12] Geffen, Rela M. Celebration and Renewal: Rites of Passage in Judaism, pg. 118.

[13] Biale, Rachel. Women and Jewish Law: The Essential Texts, Their History, and Their Relevance for Today. pg. 190

[14] Kyle Harper, "Porneia: The Making of a Christian Sexual Norm"

[15] Article: "Sergius and Bacchus: Paired male saints loved each other in ancient Roman army." https://qspirit.net/sergius-bacchus-paired-male-saints/

[16] Adaped from Matthew Vines book God and the Gay Christian.

[17] Adapted this illustration from Matthew J. Distefano's book Heretic: *An LGBTQ-Affirming, Divine Violence-Denying, Christian Universalist's Responses to Some of Evangelical Christianity's Most Pressing Concerns.*

The Way Forward

[1] Martin, Colby. UnClobber: Rethinking Our Misuse of the Bible on Homosexuality. E-book ed., Westminster John Knox Press, 2016. Kindle.

[2] Venn-Brown, Anthony, A Life of Unlearning (New Holland Publishers, 2004)

[3] https://wouldjesusdiscriminate.org/biblical_evidence/born_gay.html

[4] Lucian, Volume III (William Heinemann, London, 1921), translated by A.M. Harmon, page 197.

[5] Quintus Curtius, History of Alexander, Volume II (Harvard University Press, Cambridge, 1956), translated by John C. Rolfe, page 51.

[6] Mark Brustman. "Born Eunuchs: Homosexual Identity in the Ancient World.
https://people.well.com/user/aquarius/contents.htm

[7] These bullet points are taken from The Reformation Project website. Matthew Vines does an excellent job of summarizing the case for LGBT inclusion. Visit www.reformationproject.org for more information.

[8] Anthony Venn-Brown, 5447

Where I Am Today

[1] Some of these insights were adapted from Anthony Venn-Brown's book *A Life of Unlearning*. He had a similar path as I did, serving as a pastor. What's interesting is that we both ended up coming to the same conclusions about ourselves, God, and our Faith.

[2] McVey, Julie. Why I Left the Church to Find Jesus (Strong Oak Press, 2019), 68.

ABOUT THE AUTHOR

Dr. Brandon Park is a motivational speaker, corporate trainer, personal growth author, and life coach. He has earned two masters degrees and a doctorate from Liberty University. Brandon is the author of several other books including *The Five Essentials of Life* and *Communicate to Captivate*. He is a single father of three amazing children and they reside in Overland Park, Kansas.

To schedule Dr. Park to speak at your next event, email at brandon@brandonpark.org or visit his website at BrandonPark.org.

To schedule a coaching session, visit www.iLifeCoach.org

Printed in Great Britain
by Amazon

36677344R10136